RE-RELEASED WITH UPDATED ST

101 INCREDIBLE MOMENTS IN TENNIS

TENNIS'S BEST, TENNIS'S WORST, AND TENNIS'S MOST INFAMOUS MOMENTS

JOSHUA SHIFRIN

Printed in the United States of America

Front Cover Images: The Press Association

For my wife, Maya, and our two beautiful sons.

Acknowledgements

Joshua Shifrin

Tennis has always been my passion. From playing to watching, I am truly consumed by every aspect of the game. Consequently, as I was writing *101 Incredible Moments in Tennis* I considered it a labour of love, and as I look back on the experience I can honestly say I enjoyed every minute. However, as with any worthwhile endeavour, success is normally not achieved without the assistance of others. Such is the case with this book.

First and foremost, I want to express my gratitude to my father. From the first story he has been my biggest supporter and most arduous reviewer. He has helped me in countless ways, with every aspect of this experience, and for that I am deeply grateful.

I also want to thank my mother for being my biggest fan, and for cultivating my love of the sport by dragging me to the seemingly hundreds of tennis tournaments throughout my youth. Thank you to my high school and college coaches, Bill Kirkpatrick and Melissa Abbott, respectively, for inspiring me to make the most out of my tennis experiences, as well as to my college teammate and friend, Jordan Pinsky, for listening to me complain about my forehand for the last 25 years.

And last, but definitely not least, I want to thank my wife, Maya, and our two sons for putting up with the hours and hours of time spent working on this book, and for listening and sympathising as I rode the publishing express roller coaster.

101 Incredible Moments in Tennis

Tennis's Best, Tennis's Worst, and Tennis's Most Infamous Moments

I love tennis. I love everything about it. From the anticipation of my weekend match to lacing up my sneakers. From the *swoosh* of opening up a new can of tennis balls, to the *thwack* of the ball hitting the strings on the sweet spot of the racquet. From slices to topspin, from an explosive overhead to a delicate drop shot. Is there anything better than watching a perfectly struck topspin lob sail over your opponent's head, leaving him completely befuddled, and continuing to relish your shot as it drops two feet inside the baseline for a clean winner? And then, after you've given it your all, left it all on the court, the sweat, guts and glory (you pick the cliché), sitting back with your opponent, having a drink, and discussing the intricacies of the match. I just love it all!

And then there are the professionals. The best in the world that our great sport has to offer. Inconceivably, watching two gladiators smacking around that little yellow fuzzy ball at the highest level brings me, at times, more enjoyment, *if that's possible*, than playing myself. These incredibly talented men and women, with their livelihoods on the line, and all the pressure that goes along with it, playing their hearts out in front of, at times, millions of people, have produced some of the most riveting, unforgettable moments in all of sports. Some good moments, some great moments, and some...well...not so great moments. And although Forrest Gump might say, 'Tennis is like a box of chocolates, you never know what you're gonna get', one thing is for certain; when the question is asked, 'What do you get when you put some of the world's greatest tennis players under enormous pressure with all of the competitive juices flowing in a battle on the court?', the answer is: *101 Incredible Moments in Tennis.*

Contents

White On White

Anne White v. Pam Shriver

Tennis's 101st most incredible moment occurred at Wimbledon in 1985. As most tennis fans know, Wimbledon is nothing if not rich in tradition. From its years of history to the royal box, punctilious scheduling and verdant grass courts, Wimbledon exudes dignity and decorum. And then there is the matter of tennis's lily whites. Since the tournament's inception in 1877, Wimbledon has insisted on white tennis attire. Of course the players and officials all know the rules, but as they say, 'rules are meant to be broken'...or in this case, bent to their breaking point.

This brings us to the first-round match between well-known Pam Shriver and the soon-to-be well-known Anne White. White, a tall blonde ranked 93rd in the world, was not given much of a chance to defeat the considerably higher ranked Shriver. But playing on Court No. 2, known as the 'upset court', White was about to upset many in the Wimbledon community. It appeared to be just another wet, soggy evening on the grounds.

And then it happened...suddenly White appeared on the court wearing an *all white, skin-tight body suit*. The stir around the grounds was immediate. Fans and photographers raced to the match to catch a glimpse of White's Wimbledon fashion statement. A circus-like atmosphere ensued but even at Wimbledon 'the show must go on'.

Shriver won the first set 6–3, but White fought back to take the second set in a tiebreaker before the match was postponed due to darkness. When the women came out the following day to finish the match, White was dressed in traditional tennis whites. What happened to the body suit you may ask? Well, it appears that the Wimbledon officials deemed White's skin tights as 'not traditional tennis attire' and banned the outfit. Subsequently, White lost the match in the final set. And although Shriver called the outfit 'stupid' and 'bizarre', and ESPN eventually called the outfit the 'Worst Uniform of the Century', White went on to say, 'I didn't want anybody to spill their strawberries and cream but I think I showed a lot of guts.'

White was ranked as high as 19th in the world in singles and ninth in doubles in a very respectable career in which she amassed over one million dollars (600,000 pounds). She also was a two-time All American at the University of Southern California, and was named as one of West Virginia's top 50 greatest sports figures between 1900–2000 by *Sports Illustrated*. Quite impressive, don't you think? But to this day if you ask any tennis fan what they remember most about Anne White's tennis career, undoubtedly the first thing that will come to mind is that infamous rainy day at Wimbledon in 1985 when White shook up the establishment and gave us an incredible tennis moment to remember... Thanks, Anne.

I'll Have the Chilean Special

Nicholas Massu

Tennis's 100th most incredible moment occurred at the 2004 Olympic Games in Athens, Greece. In the 108-year history of the Olympic Games, the South American country of Chile had never won a single gold medal. However, the patriotic Chilean, Nicholas Massu, hoped to change all of that. Massu, who was born on 10 October 1979 in Vina de Mar, Chile, was a tennis player who was most at home on the slow red clay courts indigenous to his home country. Unfortunately for Nicholas, the tennis at the Athens games was being held on hard courts. And to make things even more ominous for Massu, his 2004 record on the cement-like surface coming into the Olympics was a dismal 0 and 7.

Yet as the tournament got underway something interesting began to happen. For one, Massu ended his hard court losing streak to win his first couple of rounds in both singles and doubles with his partner Fernando Gonzalez. And to further bolster the Chilean's spirits, the dominant two players in the world, Roger Federer and Andy Roddick, lost in the second and third rounds, respectively. And incredibly, as the singles and doubles draws continued to play themselves out, Massu and Gonzalez found themselves in the singles semi-final as well as the doubles final. Unfortunately for Gonzalez, his gold medal run ended abruptly with a loss to the American Mardy Fish but his compatriot, Massu, took out another American, Taylor Dent, to move into the singles final.

The good news for Gonzales was that he still had a chance to fight Dent for the Bronze medal. Making the most of his opportunity, he gained a thrilling 6-4, 2-6, 16-14 victory in a marathon three hours and 25 minutes. Yet Gonzalez didn't have much time to celebrate because later that night he had to prepare himself for the doubles final with his partner, Massu. The Chileans were trying to make history for their proud country, but to do so they would have to defeat the German team of Rainer Schuettler and Nicholas Kiefer.

The finals started off well enough for Massu and Gonzalez as they took the first set 6-2. But the tide quickly turned and the Germans took the next two sets 6-4, 6-3. When Schuettler and Keifer took a six points to two lead in the fourth-set tiebreaker it was all but over.

And then it happened...Massu and Gonzales held off one match point, then another, and another, and ultimately a fourth match point, incredibly taking the tiebreaker nine points to seven. And even after falling behind three games to one in the final set it seemed that destiny was on their side. After three hours and 43 minutes the Chileans fought back once again to take the final set 6-4 and in doing so captured their country's first ever Olympic gold medal at 2:40 am.

But for Massu there was still more work to be done. Although he didn't get to sleep until 6:30 in the morning, a drained Massu dragged himself to the singles final against the talented and rested American, Mardy Fish. Despite his fatigue Massu came out *en fuego*, winning the first five games of the match before taking the opening set 6-3. But soon weariness began to take its toll and Massu looked like a beaten man when he dropped the next two sets 6-3, 6-2. Despite this, he recognised that the opportunity facing him was once in a lifetime and he summoned his energy to take the fourth set 6-3.

Then, when Massu broke Fish's serve in the final set, he had the finish line in sight. In what can only be described as a herculean effort, Massu continued to fight on fumes. While serving for the gold at 5-4 in the fifth he finally seized match point.

And then it happened again...after a tournament that saw Massu play 24 hours and 43 minutes of physically demanding, heart-wrenching tennis, Fish hit the final shot wide as Massu fell to the court in utter

Excuse Me Sir...Or Is It Madam?

Renee Richards

Tennis's 99th most incredible moment officially occurred in 1976, but in reality was a lifetime in the making. It all started with a promising young man named Richard Raskind. As a youth, Richard was an all-round sports star who was actually scouted by the New York Yankees. He eventually concentrated on the game of tennis, achieving a level worthy of competing in the US Championship in 1955. Richard went on to medical school where he became an ophthalmologist and eventually served as an officer in the US Navy. Certainly an impressive CV on its own merit. But Richard had more in store for us. Fast forward to 1975 and meet Dr Renee Richards, formerly Dr Richard Raskind. That's right, after going under the surgeon's knife – *tadaa* – Richard became Renee.

And then it happened...In 1976 Richard/Renee started off her second career as a tennis professional. But this time *she* did it on the *women's* tennis circuit. Needless to say, it didn't take long for the controversy to begin. The Women's Tennis Association was not very happy, to say the least, that a former man wanted to compete against the women of the WTA. They argued, naturally, that a former man had an unfair advantage competing against women in the world of sports, even after legally becoming a woman himself/herself. The debate made its way all the way to the New York Supreme Court where it was decided that after a full sexual reassignment surgery, a transsexual was legally the new sex. In other words, Richards had the legal right to play professional tennis as a woman. And finally, 22 years after playing in the men's US Championship as Richard Raskind, Renee Richards played in the Women's US Open in 1977. Renee eventually reached as high as number 22 in the world on the women's tour (a ranking that far exceeded that of his male professional playing days) and reached the 1977 US Open doubles final with Betty Ann Stuart. The unusual circumstances prompt the tongue in cheek observation that it was more of a 'mixed' doubles final rather than a women's final. All in all, Richard/Renee presented the sports world with a dilemma that would give King Solomon a royal headache, and was more than noteworthy as tennis's 99th most incredible moment.

Let's Get This Party Started

Spencer Gore v. William Marshall

Tennis's 98th most incredible moment occurred at Wimbledon in 1877. The origins of tennis go back many centuries. It is said that tennis can trace its roots all the way back to ancient Egypt and Greece. Furthermore, many historical annals have proven that tennis was a game favoured by the royalties of France and England as far back as the fourteenth century. Yet it wasn't until Major Walter Clopton Wingfield of England patented tennis in 1874 that the world was given the gift of the modern game. Although the rules have varied over the years, the crux of tennis has remained the same ever since. Now I'm sure even the most casual of tennis fans are aware that Wimbledon is one of the most prestigious tournaments that our sport has to offer. Yet many fans are probably not aware that it wasn't always this way. At first, Wimbledon was not a tennis venue at all. It was originally called the All England Croquet Club, and it wasn't until 1868 that one court was assigned for tennis. And it wasn't until 1877 that the first Wimbledon tennis tournament was played.

The original tournament had a draw of only 22 men and a total audience of just 200 patrons who shelled out one shilling each to view the festivities. Although those present had no way of knowing it at the time, this event turned out to be a milestone in sports history. As the tournament progressed with lacklustre play, two men finally emerged in the finals.

And then it happened…Spencer Gore of England, a newcomer to the sport, used a serve-and-volley game, volleying winner after winner to defeat William Marshall by the score of 6-1, 6-2, 6-4 to become the first ever Grand Slam champion, thereby securing his name in the history of tennis. Ironically, Gore was not a big fan of the game, and even stated after his victory, 'It [tennis] is boring and will never catch on.' After Gore attempted to defend his championship the following year, losing in the finals, he gave up the game for good. And although it may now be apparent that Spencer Gore was not exactly what we would call a tennis visionary in 1877, he will always have the distinction of being the first Wimbledon champion.

Father Knows Best?

Damir Dokic

Tennis's 97th most incredible moment occurred on 30 August 2000 at the US Open. The stories of out-of-control fathers trying to live out their own unfulfilled dreams through their children are legendary. From verbal tongue-lashings to physical abuse, it seems that some fathers never learn. And unfortunately, tennis dads are not exempt from the list. In fact, if truth be told, they have proven to be some of the most egregious examples of this ugly side of sport. From the days of Charles Lenglen withholding the jam on his daughter Suzanne's bread for having a poor practice session, to Mary Pierce's father Jim instructing his daughter to 'kill the bitch' during her matches, it appears that the tirading tennis father will always hold an infamous position in our beautiful sport. And sadly, if recent history is any indication, the problem is only getting worse. From Stefano Capriati to Marinko Lucic to Peter Graf to Richard Williams, the archetypal tennis father is most likely here to stay. But in my opinion, if you're searching for the ultimate offender, the worst of the worst, the Big Daddy of all Bad Dads, one has to look no further than Damir Dokic.

Dokic, who was born and raised in Serbia, raised his daughter, Jelena, to be a tennis champion from the moment she could hold a racquet. And despite the fact that Jelena became one of the world's premier women players, Damir, who acted as Jelena's coach, cannot seem to stay out of trouble. For example, in June of 1999, after getting drunk and being verbally abusive during one of his daughter's matches in Birmingham, he was kicked off the grounds. In protest, the self-destructive Mr. Dokic laid himself down in the middle of the road, disrupting traffic. Then, the following year in his adopted country at the Australian Open, Damir was cited for physically assaulting a cameraman covering the event. Several months later, Mr Dokic was escorted off the grounds at Wimbledon after getting drunk once again, and this time destroying a cell phone that belonged to one of the broadcasters. After getting reprimanded at two of the year's Grand Slam events, one might think that Mr. Dokic would be on his best behaviour at the year's final slam, the US Open...Well, think again. As if saving his best – or is it his worst – for last, this time Damir wasn't even near a tennis court but simply having a little snack in the player's lounge.

And then it happened...Damir became infuriated when his expensive piece of salmon was not up to his expectations. After unleashing a verbal barrage on the unsuspecting food server, Dokic was once again escorted off the grounds by security for the third time in the year's four Grand Slam events. Still, Damir hadn't learned his lesson. In fact, he attempted to re-enter the complex via a 'players only' area. This time, as his tearful daughter looked on, he shouted profanities while being escorted from the grounds. Threatened with arrest, Damir finally got the hint and left the premises. Two weeks later the Women's Tennis Association banned Damir Dokic from attending WTA tour events for six months.

And to think that tennis was originally considered a game to be played by gentlemen and ladies. Oh, how times have changed.

From the Depths of Despair

Jennifer Capriati v. Martina Hingis

Tennis's 96th most incredible moment occurred at the 2001 Australian Open. Jennifer Marie Capriati was a tennis prodigy like no other. Born on 29 March 1976, Jennifer, like Jelena Dokic (see incredible moment #97), was groomed by her father, Stefano, to be a tennis champion seemingly from birth. As her incredible talent began to blossom, the sports world stood up and took notice. Out of the numerous newspaper, magazine and television stories chronicling Capriati's amazing journey, one summed it up best. Young Jennifer's photo appeared on the cover of *Sports Illustrated* before she ever played a professional tournament with the caption, 'She's Only 13'. With the fanfare of a superstar, Capriati turned pro on 5 March 1990 just before her 14th birthday and unbelievably made it all the way to the finals of her first tournament. While most girls her age were trying to figure out what to wear to school, Jennifer was getting paid millions in endorsements to wear cute tennis outfits.

Things seemingly began effortlessly for Jen. After one year on the tour she was already in the top ten in the world. She then won the Olympic gold in Barcelona in 1992. But as one tournament turned into the next, the expectations on the girl deemed to be the future of American tennis grew larger and larger. Unfortunately, the incredible pressure eventually overwhelmed her. After being arrested for shoplifting, Capriati had her mug shot posted all over the world when she was picked up for possession of approximately 20 grams of marijuana in Florida in 1994.

At this point Capriati had had enough. Although she had planned to take a break from the trials and tribulations of the tour following the 1993 US Open, the 'break' ended up being a two-and-a-half year layoff. When she finally returned to the tour in 1996 the fragile Capriati was a shell of her former tennis self. But the resilient American, with the heart of a champion, fought to regain her past form. After working herself back into top shape, Jennifer began to slowly move up the tennis ladder. By the time the 2001 Australian Open rolled around, Capriati was able to secure a number 12 seed. Not exactly what the Capriati of old was accustomed to, but respectable nevertheless. But then something unexpected started to happen. Capriati began to find her game. As she worked her way through the opening rounds, her game grew stronger with every victory. But it wasn't until she defeated the highly ranked Lindsay Davenport that the tennis critics were truly impressed. And then, when she defeated the four-time champ Monica Seles in the semis, the 24-year-old Capriati had reached her first Grand Slam final ten years after joining the tour.

Unfortunately for Jennifer, it looked like the gravy train was about to drop her off short of her ultimate destination. Not only was the top-seeded Martina Hingis waiting for her in the finals, but Hingis had already beaten both of the powerful Williams sisters for the first time in the same tournament. Hence, Hingis was a heavy favourite. But apparently no one told Capriati that she was supposed to lie down and play dead. Jennifer shot out of the gates to a 4-0 lead in a crackling 12 minutes. And although Hingis mounted a comeback, Jen was able to hold her off and win the first set 6-4. The second set started off tighter than the first but when Hingis double-faulted on break point to go down 3-2, Capriati was poised to accomplish the improbable. As the women continued to hold serve, Capriati was on the verge of fulfilling the expectations of years gone by. Jennifer Marie Capriati was serving at 5-4 with a championship point.

And then it happened...Capriati ripped a backhand up the line for a clean winner and it was over. Capriati had done it! Ten years after joining the tour as a teenage phenomenon, she had shocked the tennis world. As Jennifer received her first Grand Slam trophy she summed it up best when she told the ecstatic, sold out stadium crowd, 'Who would've thought I would have ever made it here after so much has happened? Dreams do come true if you keep believing in yourself. Anything can happen.'

As an encore, Capriati backed up her first Grand Slam title by winning her second major just four months later at the French Open. And as if that wasn't enough, she backed that up by becoming only the ninth woman to hold the number one ranking since the women's computer rankings began on 3 November 1975.

Scandal!

Nicolay Davydenko v. Martin Vassallo Arguello

Tennis's 95th most incredible moment occurred on 2 August 2007. Nicolay Davydenko was born on 2 June 1981 in Severodonetsk, Ukraine. Recognised as a tennis talent early in life, he soon achieved success, and by most standards he has had a very impressive career. For several years he has been entrenched in the world's top five, having reached four Grand Slam semi-finals to date (French Open in 2005, 2007 and US Open 2006, 2007). Nicolay is known for his quickness, powerful baseline game, and for playing more matches per year than any other player on tour. Hence, his hard-earned nickname, 'Iron Man'. Despite these credentials, however, for most of his career he has been best known for being unknown. Other players with a 'name', like Andy Roddick, James Blake and Andy Murray, were often ranked below Davydenko, but while they were riding a crest of popularity and lucrative endorsements, Nicolay continued to labour in relative anonymity. Perhaps this was because of his workmanlike demeanour or his basic lack of star quality, but in any case, the Davydenko image has somehow remained well under the media radar.

And then it happened... after a rare slump in which he lost three first-round matches in a row, Nicolay entered a seemingly low-profile tournament in Sopot, Poland, where his first-round opponent was the unknown Martin Vassallo Arguello. After the heavily favoured Davydenko won the first set 6-2, several inexplicable and extremely large wagers were placed with Betfair, a gambling company, in favour of...you guessed it, Arguello! Subsequently, Davydenko lost the second set, and in the third he withdrew with an injury, handing the victory to Arguello on a platter.

Upon investigation it was revealed that over seven million dollars (four million pounds) was wagered, ten times the typical amount for a competition of this nature. Betfair immediately reported the incident to the Association of Tennis Professional and voided all bets. Let the circus begin! As a cloud of controversy hung over Davydenko's head he continued to proclaim his complete innocence. While there have been lesser-known match-fixing controversies in the past, none had gained the notoriety or endured as long as the Davydenko-Arguello incident.

Many were of the opinion that Davydenko should be suspended during the investigation. The ATP chose to allow him to compete, however, and despite the intense scrutiny, Nicolay toughed it out and performed quite well, reaching the US Open semi-finals just one month after being accused. The inquiry continued for over a year, however, until finally, on 11 September 2008, both Davydenko and Arguello were cleared of all charges.

While Nicolay Davydenko had been trying to make a name for himself in a career that was heretofore unheralded, one can assume that this was not his preferred method for grabbing the spotlight. With his prodigious talent, he still has the potential to re-establish his legacy through outstanding play on the court.

For now, despite his innocent verdict, the first thing that comes to mind for many fans is the infamous 2007 betting scandal that rocked the tennis world. But don't think for a minute that this is going to slow him down. There's plenty to come from Nicolay Davydenko. You can bet on it!

A Tennis Tragedy

Stefan Edberg and Linesman Dick Wertheim

Tennis's 94th most incredible moment occurred during the 1983 US Open junior boys final. Stefan Edberg had a tennis career that was paralleled by few others. Born on 19 January 1966 in the small town of Vastervik, Sweden, Stefan Edberg first picked up a racquet at the tender age of seven. Little Stefan showed an immediate talent for the game and won his first big junior tournament at the age of 12. Edberg's junior career was brilliant. He won one important title after another, and at the age of 16 he won one of the most prestigious junior title in tennis, the Orange Bowl in Florida. But it was in 1983 that he made history. Edberg started off the junior Grand Slam season by winning the French Open. He then made his way to Wimbledon where he took the boys title there as well. Edberg was now half way to the junior Grand Slam, a feat that had never been accomplished. He then advanced to the US Open junior finals where he was the favourite to win the title.

And then it happened...during the match the 17-year-old Edberg unleashed one of his patented hard serves right up the middle. Regrettably, the serve hit the centreline judge, Dick Wertheim, in the groin. Wertheim, reeling from the blow, fell forward and struck his head on the court. Although he was rushed to a nearby Flushing Meadow, New York hospital, he had suffered a brain haemorrhage and never regained consciousness. In a devastating turn of events, Wertheim died at the age of 61.

Edberg went on to win the match and followed that up with an Australian Open victory to become the only junior ever to win the junior Grand Slam to date. He would go on to win six professional Grand Slam singles titles and 41 professional singles titles in all, achieve a number one world ranking in singles and doubles, and earn more than 20 million dollars (12 million pounds) in a Hall of Fame career. Yet it was the quirky, tragic accident on that one unfortunate day in 1983 that resulted in the 94th most incredible moment in tennis history.

What's a Couple of Feet Between Friends?

Anne Kremer v. Jennifer Hopkins

Tennis's 93rd most incredible moment occurred at the 2002 Bausch & Lomb Women's Championships in Amelia Island, Florida. It has been said that for every athlete at the top of their sport there are thousands of other hopefuls vying for that elite status. For every Martina Navratilova or Serena Williams, there is a plethora of young women who are literally sleeping in their cars, just looking to scrounge out a career.

Two such women are Anne Kremer and Jennifer Hopkins. Although neither woman had a stellar ranking, both were united in the dream of making that major breakthrough into the upper echelon of the Women's Tennis Association rankings. And when Kremer and Hopkins met in the first round of the prestigious Bausch & Lomb Championships, undoubtedly both women saw it as a major chance to take a step towards their dreams. The players stepped out onto the stadium court to play the opening match of the tournament. After they took their allotted five minute warm-up, the chair umpire made her announcement, 'Players ready. Play.'

And then it happened...one double fault, two double faults, three double faults, and on and on it went. As Kremer and Hopkins battled throughout the match their serving woes continued. As the match finally, mercifully concluded with a 5-7, 6-4, 6-2 Kremer victory, the women had racked up an astronomical 29 combined double faults. Kremer had served

16 double faults, and not to be outdone, Hopkins had thrown in 13 service miscues of her own. After the match, the two women, who assumed that they had not both forgotten how to serve at the same time, sensed something was awry and complained to tournament officials. As a result the court was measured, and sure enough, it was discovered that the service lines were only 18 feet from the net as opposed to the 21 foot required distance. The service lines were three feet too short!

How could this happen? The head of court maintenance, Bert Evatt, who has been lining the courts for 22 years succinctly stated, 'I screwed up. I flip-flopped the distances. It is supposed to be 21 from the net to the service line and then 18 feet to the baseline. I made it 18 and 21.' After deliberating for six hours the WTA officials stated that the match would not be replayed and Kremer would remain the winner.

I've heard of a 'home court', advantage but in this case it appears that Kremer benefited from a 'short court' advantage. Now that's one for the books...or at least this book.

Tummy Ache

Justine Henin v. Amelie Mauresmo

Tennis's 92nd most incredible moment occurred at the 2006 Australian Open Women's Final. Justine Henin is often considered to be one of the most talented players ever to play the game. With beautiful, flowing ground strokes, solid net play, a powerful serve, and the quickness of a cat, Henin has often been referred to as the female Roger Federer. In addition, she has that extra quality that separates the great ones from the rest of the pack: a killer instinct. On many occasions Henin has relied on her legendary tenacity to tough out one perilous situation after another. Using her rare combination of mental strength and physical genius, she has propelled herself to seven career Grand Slam singles titles as well as the 2004 Olympic gold medal. Consequently, during the 2006 Australian Open, Henin was considered an excellent candidate to walk away with the champion's trophy.

As the year's first Grand Slam got underway, Henin appeared to grow stronger as the tournament progressed. She breezed through the draw, defeating top-ranked Lindsay Davenport along the way, and continued on her determined path to the championship round by ousting the imposing Maria Sharapova in the semis. In fact, Henin was playing so well that going into the final she was quoted as saying that she was at the 'peak of my fitness' and that she was playing the 'best tennis of my life'. And in case there remained any doubt about the outcome, Justine's opponent in the final was the popular but inconsistent Amelie Mauresmo. Like Henin, Mauresmo was immensely talented. And at 5′ 9″ tall, broad shouldered and a solid 150 pounds (68 kilos), she was also a far more imposing physical specimen than the 5′ 6″, waif-like Henin. But Mauresmo had a glaring Achilles heel, a tendency to wilt under the intense spotlight of big time tennis. The popular French star had been to four previous Grand Slam semi-finals as well as the championship round in the 1999 Australian Open, but in each and every attempt she had fallen in defeat. In fact, in 2004 she briefly held the world's number one ranking despite having no Grand Slam titles in her record, and had been described as the best player on the women's tour never to have won a major.

But, surprise! As the match started, the unexpected began to unfold. Mauresmo shot out of the gate like a thoroughbred, and by the time the spectators had settled in their seats, she had raced through the first set, 6-1. The tennis-savvy Aussie crowd was stunned. Surely this was a fluke. Henin, the great Belgian fighter, would pull herself off the canvas and come out swinging. But, surprise again! As the second set progressed it was more of the same. Mauresmo divulged no sign of her fragile nerves, and she continued to dominate the match.

And then it happened...with Mauresmo leading 2-0 in the second set, the heavily favoured Henin walked up to the chair umpire and abruptly retired, citing severe stomach pain as the reason she could not continue. Incredibly, Justine Henin became the first woman in the history of the sport to retire in a Grand Slam final, thereby making Amelie Mauresmo the first to win a major title by default!

As Mauresmo claimed her long-sought prize, many felt that her trophy was tarnished as she won it by forfeiture. But in yet another surprise, Amilie backed it up later that same year by winning tennis's most coveted Grand Slam title, the championship at Wimbledon. And she did so by prevailing in an exhilarating three-set final, defeating none other than...you guessed it...the incomparable Justine Henin!

Black Jack

Vince Spadea

Tennis's 91st most incredible moment occurred during the 2000 season. Yet this story really started on 19 July 1974 when Vincent and Hilda Spadea gave birth to a baby boy named Vincent Spadea Jr. From a very young age Vince showed great promise as a budding tennis prodigy, turning his talent and hard work into a stellar junior career. In 1988, at the age of 14, Vince won six junior national titles. And then in 1992 he became the first American junior to win the prestigious Orange Bowl tournament in Miami Beach, Florida since Jim Courier had done so in 1987.

Vince entered the professional ranks in 1993, and like his junior results, he found immediate success. In his first professional match he defeated one of the world's top players, Andres Gomez. By the end of 1994 Vince was the youngest American player to finish out the year ranked in the top 100. Continuing to show promise as he clawed his way up the professional ranks, he eventually cracked the world's top twenty for the first time on 13 September 1999.

And then it happened...Vince lost a match, then another, and then another. As the losses began to pile up, the tennis world began to follow one of the most infamous of streaks. Eventually the highly talented athlete had lost an Associated of Tennis Professionals record 21 matches in a row...yes, 21 matches in a row! His fellow players began to playfully tease Vince by calling him 'Black Jack', and it looked like a sure 22nd loss was to follow when Vince drew the big-hitting, 14th-seeded Canadian-turned-Englishman Greg Rusedski on the fast courts of Wimbledon in the first round. It appeared so bad for Vince that he said at match time, 'My parents left and went home two days ago. I think they saw the draw and thought, Vince, man…' But as they say, that's why they play the matches. And inexplicably Spadea, who hadn't won a match since winning one in Lyon all the way back in October of 1999, pulled off one of the biggest upsets of his career by defeating Rusedski 6-3, 6-7, 6-3, 6-7, 9-7 in a war that lasted nearly four hours.

Thankfully, mercifully, the losing streak was over. Spadea would end an abysmal 2000 season with only three wins on the ATP tour and see his ranking drop 210 spots from 19th in the world all the way down to 229th. Spadea did have a career resurgence and in March 2004, in his 223rd ATP tour event, Vince actually won his first professional title. But until someone comes along and breaks it, and undoubtedly some poor unsuspecting soul will, Vincent Spadea Jr. will always be known as the holder of one of the most undesirable records in tennis…the longest losing streak in professional tennis history.

Keep Your Eyes on the Prize

Richard Krajicek v. MaliVai Washington

Tennis's 90th most incredible moment occurred at the 1996 Wimbledon final. Up until the final Sunday it had already been an incredible tournament. Richard Krajicek had pulled off the upset of the fortnight by handing three-time defending champion Pete Sampras what would be his only loss at the championships between 1993 and 2000. And for his own part, MaliVai Washington had pulled off the comeback of the tournament by fighting back from a 5-1 fifth-set deficit to defeat his countryman, Todd Martin, in the semi-finals. Krajicek and Washington were both playing their first Grand Slam final, and the setting was, of all places, the Big 'W'. As both players were standing at the net for the pre-match photographs you could cut the tension with a knife. The match of their lives was just moments away.

And then it happened... A 23-year-old Englishwoman named Melissa Johnson came streaking across Centre Court. And when I say streaking, I mean '*streaking*'. The blonde bombshell, who was a part-time Wimbledon waitress, was wearing little more than her birthday suit. As the normally sedate All England Club crowd roared its approval, both men broke into wide smiles. Washington even lifted up his own shirt in a mock show of streaker support. Eventually, order was restored and the 'real' show got underway. As it turned out, the appetiser was tastier than the main course. In a match that was interrupted by several rain delays,

Krajicek eventually won the title in straight sets 6-3, 6-4, 6-3. In the post-match interview, when Washington was asked about the effect the streaker had on his play, he responded, 'I saw these things wobbling around and jeez, she smiled at me. I was flustered. Three sets later I was gone. If she'd come back I might have had more luck.'

It is said that one learns more in defeat than victory. In MaliVai Washington's case perhaps the lesson would be, 'keep your eyes on the prize'.

The Ultimate Drubbing

Natalia Zvereva v. Steffi Graf

Tennis's 89th most incredible moment occurred during the 1988 French Open final. Natalia Zvereva was born on 16 April 1971 in Minsk, Bellarussia, and like many other tennis players around the world she dreamed of someday becoming a Grand Slam champion. Blessed with immense talent, Zvereva entered her first professional event in 1985. She gradually emerged as a contender, and by the time the French Open began in 1988, she was the 13th seed. The tournament, as they say, would be the best of times and the worst of times for the 5′ 8″ Russian right-hander. Zvereva cruised through the first three rounds of the tournament when she ran into the legendary Martina Navratilova in the fourth round. But the 17-year-old Zvereva was riding a wave of confidence and upset the second seed in straight sets. Then she continued her giant killing ways in the next round when she upset the seventh seeded Helena Sukova, once again in straight sets. And after a nail-biting victory over the unseeded Australian Nicole Provis by the score of 6-3, 6-7, 7-5 in the semi-finals, Zvereva had reached her first Grand Slam singles final. That was the good news. The bad news was that her opponent was the world's number one, Steffi Graf. Yet one must have assumed that Zvereva had as good a chance as anyone against the German powerhouse. She had already defeated two top ten players and was playing the best tennis of her life.

Well, think again. As the finals got underway Graf got off to a fast start. And a fast middle. And a fast end.

And then it happened…Graf had served up a classic drubbing in a don't-blink-or-you-could-miss-it 32 minutes. A 6-0, 6-0 pounding, the likes of which hadn't been seen in a Grand Slam final since 1911, when the British player, Dorothea Chambers, administered the worst of all drubbings to her countrywoman Dora Boothby in the Wimbledon final. After the match the shell-shocked Zvereva was quoted as saying, 'I wanted to do well but Graf was so awesome that after the first set I began to think about what I would have to eat for dinner later.' Zvereva would eventually become one of the greatest doubles players of all time by winning an astonishing 20 doubles Grand Slam titles, but she would never again reach a Grand Slam singles final. Ironically, a tournament that was in effect Zvereva's best effort in a Grand Slam will always be remembered most for the humiliating thrashing she took in the final.

Fifteen Minutes of Fame

Nick Brown v. Goran Ivanisevic

Tennis's 88th most incredible moment occurred at Wimbledon on 30 June 1991. Although many tennis players dream of what it might be like to be the next Andre Agassi or Billie Jean King, most of us have to settle for our weekend doubles game where we hack away in hopes of striking that one perfect shot. Yet even for the small percentage of players with enough talent and grit to make it to the professional level, only a fraction of the elite become champions. The larger, unnoticed majority plod along in hopes of one day making a breakthrough. These players are willing to scrounge by on peanut butter and bread, and sleep in the back of their cars, in the slim hopes of gaining their 15 minutes of fame.

One such journeyman was Nick Brown. Brown was born on 3 September 1961 in Warrington, UK. After struggling on the professional circuit for several years, he had eventually had enough and called it quits. But the thrill of competition and the thoughts of what could have been never left him. So after a five-year hiatus from the game he loved, he decided to make a comeback. Brown's previous Grand Slam experience had consisted of a first-round loss at Wimbledon in 1982. Following his return to tennis, he had actually managed to qualify for the 1989 and 1990 Wimbledon championships and the 1990 Australian Open, but his results remained the same, losing in the first round of all three events.

The good news, if there was any, was that in 1991 England had very few quality home-grown professionals. Consequently, when it came time to give out wild card entries for England's Grand Slam, the Wimbledon committee offered one of its free passes into the main draw to the 591st-ranked Nick Brown. And after years of struggle and turmoil, Brown would finally capitalise on his good fortune by winning his first-round match and his only Grand Slam singles match to date.

Unfortunately for Brown, it appeared to all that his luck had run out when his second-round opponent was none other than the huge serving, future Wimbledon champion Goran Ivanisevic (see incredible moment #28). Despite the fact that the 10th-seeded Croat was known to be streaky, his inevitable victory was about as certain as rain in London throughout the fortnight...a foregone conclusion. And after Ivanisevic won the first set 6-4 you could bet the proverbial house on Goran in a straight-sets victory. Yet it appeared that no one told Brown of his fate. In a surprise development, he came back to win the second set 6-3. And when Brown took the third set in a tiebreaker, all of England, and the tennis world, stood up and said *'Nick who?'*

And then it happened...Inconceivably, Brown took the fourth set 6-3. In doing so, the lowest-ranked man in the tournament had made his mark by pulling off the biggest upset in Wimbledon history. Brown had shocked the world...or at least the tennis viewing part of it.

Do You Have a Bus to Catch?

Suzanne Leglen v. Mary K. Browne

Tennis's 87th most incredible moment occurred at the 1926 French Open. This moment, like several others in this book, involved the legendary Suzanne Lenglen. Although Lenglen was unaware at the time, this would be her last full Grand Slam event due to the controversy of the 1926 Wimbledon Championships. (See incredible moment #72.) But oh boy, did Suzanne know how to go out with style. Lenglen's brilliant career was notorious for its dramatic flair. Whether she was drinking brandy on a changeover during matches, crying on the court, or simply showing off by unnecessarily jumping high into the air to hit one of her signature flying ground strokes, Suzanne knew how to capture one's attention. But it was on tennis's grandest stages that Lenglen shone brightest. Not only did she capture six Wimbledon singles titles, but the Frenchwoman thrilled her countrymen by winning ten French titles. In addition, Suzanne won two doubles and two mixed doubles titles to go along with her six singles championships victories. Yet by most accounts her most impressive French performance would be her last. After cruising through yet another inferior group of competitors, Lenglen reached the 1926 French Championship final.

Her opponent that day would be the estimable American Mary K. Browne. Coming into the French finals, Browne already boasted three US titles and was ranked sixth in the world. But on this day in Paris, if

Browne thought she had a chance, she was in for a rude awakening. As the match got underway, Lenglen, like clockwork, came out firing and quickly took the first set 6-1. Predictably, the second set went much the same as the first. One love, two love, three love, four love, five love, for Lenglen. But what was not so predictable was the pace at which Lenglen was racking up the games. It seemed that before the French fans could even warm up their expensive seats, the match was coming to an end.

And then it happened... Lenglen closed out the match and her sixth French Championship title by the score of 6-1, 6-0 in an eye-blinking 27 minutes. And incredibly, these mere 27 minutes have held the test of time. There has never been a quicker Grand Slam final, before or since. This Grand Slam title would prove to be the great Suzanne's last, even though her career lasted several more years. Ironically, one of Lenglen's frequent professional foes was none other than Mary K. Browne. And in case you were wondering, Lenglen's professional record versus Browne was a perfect 38-0.

The Wave

The British Crowd

Tennis's 86th most incredible moment occurred at the 1991 Wimbledon Championships. Wimbledon has been the ultimate in sophistication and refinement since its inception in 1887. From the upper echelons of society to royalty, Wimbledon has always had a snobbish quality which seems to state that its tournament, players and fans are better than all others. And in keeping with its principles of superiority, the Wimbledon committee has set up several by-laws in an apparent attempt to make sure its tournament, and the people involved with it, don't tip the delicate balance between the excitement of a world-class event and the manner in which its refined, dignified fans should behave. For example, there is the stipulation that its players dress in predominately white attire. The linesmen and lineswomen are almost always made to keep their jackets on unless the heat of the summer tournament makes it virtually unbearable. And finally, the middle Sunday of the fortnight is a day kept sacred in which they never play tennis. Yet this last rule has not always been an easy one to adhere to, because as sure as you can bet that there will be strawberries and cream at Wimbledon, you can also bet your last penny that there will be rain. And some people do. Believe it or not, of the many things that you can bet on with the London bookmakers, there is a long-shot wager that the entire two-week event will take place rain free. This gamble rarely, if ever, pays off. But there is an exception to every rule, and even the majestic Wimbledon is no exception.

In 1991, well before the retractable roof was added to Centre Court in 2009, the rain gods cast their spell on Wimbledon with a mighty fury. As the rain continued to pour day after day throughout the first week, the matches became backlogged to an unmanageable degree. Things became so precarious that by Friday the tournament committee, in its ultimate wisdom, actually decided to break with tradition and play tennis on the middle Sunday. As the tickets were quickly printed, the fans queued up in long lines to be a part of history. To add to the chaos, the day was categorised as 'open seating' on a first come, first serve basis. Consequently, when the fans were admitted to the grounds, one could really say that the flood gates opened as the excited spectators literally sprinted in to get the best seats they could. This would be a day, and a crowd, like no other in the history of the championships. As the matches got underway, the raucous crowd could hardly contain themselves.

And then it happened...as if they were at a common football or soccer game, the crowd broke out into the first 'Wave' that has ever been seen on such hallowed soil. As the patrons howled with joy and the players looked on with glee, a good time was had by all. And although many of the Wimbledon elitists may have frowned on such a boorish display, I for one was thrilled to see such a genuine outpouring of raw emotion. For let us not forget, even a game made for kings can always use a couple of jokers to keep things interesting.

Six Years In a Row!

Chris Evert

Tennis's 85th most incredible moment occurred between 1973 and 1979. (Ok, some moments are longer than others.) Christine Marie Evert was born on 21 December 1954. An indisputable prodigy from day one, Chris Evert had a tennis career which has gone down as one of the greatest of all time, illustrated by the following achievements: For 13 straight years, between 1974 and 1986, Evert won at least one Grand Slam singles event; she won 157 overall singles titles throughout her Hall of Fame career; from 1972 to 1989 she was never ranked lower than fourth in the world; between the years of 1975 to 1986 she ended the year ranked either first or second in the world; and she also won a total of 18 Grand Slam singles titles, which ties her with Martina Navratilova for fourth on the all-time list.

When Jimmy Evert was beginning to teach his young daughter Chrissie how to play the game of tennis, she was so small that she needed two hands to hold up her racquet on her backhand. When Jimmy was later asked about his daughter's two-handed backhand, which was unconventional at the time, he stated, 'I hoped she'd change, but how can I argue with success?' Evert's two-handed backhand would eventually prove to be her bread and butter. A stroke that could be hit with power and control, it soon became a standard for many who followed. The two-handed backhand has proven to be an excellent choice for hard courts, but it was the perfect shot for the slow, methodical, consistent style needed on clay. Consequently, Evert won a record seven French Open titles on the slowest of all surfaces, the red clay of Roland Garros. Although Chris Evert has created countless memorable moments on the court, incredible moment #85 started in August of 1973.

And then it happened... with a seemingly insignificant first-round clay court victory in 1973, the woman who was nicknamed the 'Ice Maiden' went on a streak that was paralleled by few others in sports. Chris Evert went on to win that tournament, and her next clay court tournament, and her next...and her next...and on and on she went. For an incredible six-year period, she did not lose a match on her favourite of surfaces. Ironically (and somewhat predictably) in May 1979 at the semi-finals of the Italian Open, Tracy Austin, one of the many 'Chrissie clones' who was following in Evert's footsteps with the two-handed backhand, finally ended this most incredible of streaks by defeating Evert 6-4, 2-6, 7-6. Although Evert would still be a force to be reckoned with for another brilliant ten years as a professional, she would never again dominate as she did for one of the most incredible six-year periods tennis has ever seen.

The Wimbledon Shocker

Lori McNeil v. Steffi Graf

Tennis's 84th most incredible moment occurred at the 1994 Wimbledon Championships. Lori McNeil was born on 18 December 1963 in San Diego, California. But after her family moved, McNeil and her future professional colleague, Zina Garrison, grew up playing together on the courts of Houston, Texas in the 1970s. As McNeil's game flourished she was finally ready to try her game on the pro circuit at the tender age of 19. For the next several years, Lori climbed her way up the rankings, eventually reaching her first big breakthrough at the 1987 US Open where she reached the semi-finals. In 1988, she achieved her highest career singles ranking at number ten in the world, and her highest doubles ranking the same year at number nine. And although McNeil remained somewhat successful, ultimately winning ten tournaments throughout her career, she struggled to find her Grand Slam magic of 1987. Truth be told, from 1988 to 1993 McNeil never advanced past the fourth round at a major. But at the 1994 Wimbledon Championships Lori's luck was about to change, although you never would have guessed it by looking at the draw. McNeil's first-round opponent was none other than the world's dominant number one player, Steffi Graf. And not only was Graf the number one seed (McNeil was unseeded), but she was also the three-time defending Wimbledon champion.

As the first-round match got underway on a cloudy and overcast Tuesday afternoon that would eventually be interrupted several times by rain, the aggressive American came out battling. McNeil's game plan was to continually attack and get to the net at every opportunity. And through the first six games of the match the plan was working to perfection as McNeil took a surprising 4-2 advantage. But Graf, a relentless competitor, predictably fought back and evened the set at five games all. Incredibly, McNeil steadied herself and continued to attack, and in a shocker she took the first set 7-5. The sold-out crowd, Steffi Graf, and most importantly, McNeil, still knew that she was a long way from pay dirt. When Graf jumped ahead five games to three with a set point in the second set, it seemed as if Lori's party might be coming to an end. But McNeil wiped away the set point with an ace, went on to hold serve, and then incredibly broke Graf's serve to even the set at five games apiece. After splitting the next two games McNeil had her chance to finish off Graf in a tiebreaker. The tiebreaker proved to be a nail-biter but McNeil held her nerve, eventually went ahead six points to five, and was about to serve with a match point.

And then it happened... McNeil put her serve cleanly into the service box, rushed the net, put away a volley, and it was over! As the 30-year-old McNeil calmly shook Graf's hand, it was if she hadn't realised the magnitude of her accomplishment. For not only had McNeil pulled off a stunning upset, but in reality it was the first time in the history of the Wimbledon Championships that a woman's number one seed had been ousted in the first round. Furthermore, Steffi Graf had not lost a Grand Slam first-round match since all the way back in 1984. But the excitement was not over for McNeil. She ultimately equalled her career Grand Slam best effort by making it all the way to the semi-finals where she lost a heart-wrenching match, 10-8 in the third, to Conchita Martinez. And although Martinez would hold up the winner's trophy at tournament's end, the 1994 Wimbledon Championships will always be remembered for Lori McNeil's incredible upset all the way back in the very first round.

What's All That Racquet?

Goran Ivanisevic v. Hyung Lee

Tennis's 83rd most incredible moment occurred at the Samsung Open in Brighton, in 2000. For several years many tennis journalists and fans alike had criticised the men's tour for being too benign, for lacking emotion. 'Where are all of the personalities of yesteryear?' they protest. 'What happened to the days when the players used to wear their hearts on their sleeves?' 'Where are the McEnroes, Connors and Nastasies!' However, even the most vehement protestors must grudgingly admit that today's brand of tennis does serve up several colourful characters. For example, Rafael Nadal has never been labelled as boring. And Andy Murray has been known to speak his mind on several occasions. But if outlandish behaviour is your thing, you need look no further than Croatia's Goran Ivanisevic. Ever since Ivanisevic was a young boy, playing in what was then Yugoslavia, he always let it all hang out. If he was happy, you'd know it. If he was upset, you'd definitely know it. Goran was an open book for the world to see. He was the quintessential extrovert and things didn't change when he joined the professional tour. As a result, he was constantly being warned and fined for his outlandish behaviour. Goran has seemingly racked up enough money in fines to feed a small country. Yet it was at the 2000 Samsung Open where Ivanisevic reached his all-time low – or high – depending on whom you're talking to.

In his first-round match an incident foreshadowed things to come.

After a stout lineswoman reported Goran for using profanity, Ivanisevic retorted, 'What is your problem? Is it weight?' But after cooling down enough to win the match, Goran embarked on a course in the second round that would lead to a well-deserved reputation for infamy. His first mistake, as any reputable boy scout will tell you, is that the Croat was not prepared. While players normally come onto the court with eight to ten racquets, Goran showed up with only three. When he began his match against Korea's Hyung Lee, all seemed to be under control. But when Ivanisevic lost a crucial service game at 5-5 in the first set, he slammed his racquet to the court, leaving him with two racquets for the rest of the match. After Lee held serve to take the first set, Goran regained control and took an uneventful second set in a tiebreaker. But at one all in the third, Goran blew a couple of break point opportunities. Apparently blaming the racquet for his poor play, he let his weapon have it. And then there was one. And incredibly, in the very next game, Goran double faulted and you guessed it. *Smash*...and then there were none. As Goran came to his senses it dawned on him that there was nothing left to play with. After he was unable to locate another one of his Head Prestige Classic 600 racquets, the tournament supervisor Gerry Armstrong had only one viable solution.

And then it happened...Armstrong made the precedent-setting decision to default Ivanisevic for 'lack of appropriate equipment'. For the first time in the history of a major ATP event, a player had to be disqualified for lacking a racquet! And considering that Goran not only gets his equipment for free, but actually gets paid a significant fee to use them, this story definitely made a lot of racquet.

Take That, Old Man

Jimmy Connors v. Ken Rosewall

Tennis's 82nd most incredible moment occurred in the 1974 US Open final. In 1974 Jimmy Connors was not only a brash, young, upstart American, but he was also the world's best player. By the end of the year Connors had won an incredible 99 of 103 matches and turned those victories into 15 tournament titles. And despite the fact that Jimmy's whole year could be considered an incredible moment, this particular episode occurred during the year's American Grand Slam, the US Open. Coming into 'The Open', as it has come to be known, Connors had become ill. In fact he had a virus and some felt that he might not even be able to compete. Yet despite fatigue and weight loss, Connors was up to the challenge. Jimmy fought through the draw with his typical guts, tears and sweat, and when he beat fellow American Roscoe Tanner in the semis he was ready for a repeat of the Wimbledon final with an ageing but game Ken Rosewall.

Although many younger fans may not know it, Jimmy was not always the fan favourite he was to become at the latter stages of his career. In fact, in 1974 he was considered to be the prototypical bad boy and it was Rosewall, who would be 40 by year's end, who was the overwhelming sentimental favourite. Yet despite the partisan crowd, Connors must have felt confident after having destroyed Rosewall months earlier at the Big 'W' (see incredible moment #60). But if Rosewall or his fans were hoping that history would not repeat itself, they were sadly mistaken. As the match got underway it seemed as if Rosewall could do no right and Jimmy no wrong. Connors took the first set 6-1 and steamrolled Rosewall 6-0 in the second.

And then it happened...before the crowd could say, 'How much did we pay for these tickets?' Jimbo had taken the third set and the title, 6-1, in the most one-sided drubbing a US Open final has ever seen. As it turned out, Connors missed his chance to become only the third man in history to win the Grand Slam, when the French Federation banned him from playing in the French Open because he played World Team Tennis. But in the 1974 US Open final, James Scott Connors, Jr. would write his own history, and it appears as if Jimmy fancies short stories.

Battle of the Big Babes

Venus Williams v. Lindsay Davenport

Tennis's 81st most incredible moment occurred at the 2005 Wimbledon Ladies final. The participants were the current world's number one player, Lindsay Davenport, and former number one, Venus Williams. While the combatants may have appeared to be dissimilar, in actuality they had a lot in common. Both women were born and grew up playing in California. They were both over six feet tall with powerful games to match. They were both previous Wimbledon champions. And most importantly, it had been years since either woman had enjoyed a Grand Slam title. Consequently, when Williams and Davenport walked out onto Centre Court for the final, they were both desperate for victory.

As the match got underway, it was Lindsay who started off quickly, jumping out to a five games to two advantage. But just in case Davenport thought she was in for a walk in the park, Venus turned up the heat by taking the next eight points, to narrow the gap to five games to four. Now with the set tightening Davenport showed her own resolve and steadied herself to serve out the first set six games to four.

The second set was also closely contested as Davenport finally broke to go ahead 6-5 and had the opportunity to serve for the championship. Yet as she would do throughout the final, Williams would play her best tennis with her back against the wall. She quickly broke back at love and carried her momentum through the tiebreaker to take the second set.

It was now one set for all the marbles and both women would give it everything they had. As the final set played itself out the tension was unbearable. And finally, with Davenport leading five games to four, Williams tossed in a double fault to give Lindsay a match point.

And then it happened...With the title slipping away, Venus summoned up all of her considerable courage and ripped a backhand winner to stave off match point, and went on to hold serve. Two games later it was six all. With no tiebreaker in the final set at Wimbledon, the women would battle on. Then at seven games apiece, Williams finally broke serve and had the match on her racquet. After trailing for almost the entire final, Venus wasn't going to let the chance slip away. At 40-15 Davenport's final forehand missed its mark and it was over. After two hours and 45 minutes, the longest women's final in the history of the championships, Williams had done it. In securing her third Wimbledon crown, Venus became the lowest seeded player to win the title at number 14. Furthermore, she was the first woman in 70 years to win Wimbledon after facing a match point. But most dramatically of all, Venus Williams had resurrected her career by pulling off one of the most thrilling Wimbledon victories in the history of the Championships.

Gorgeous Gussy

Gertrude Moran

Tennis's 80th most incredible moment occurred at the 1949 Wimbledon Championships. The 1949 tournament will always be remembered for Ted 'Lucky' Schroeder's amazing title run. (See incredible moment #62.) Yet the story line that stole the show was a little ol' pair of lace-trimmed knickers. Although something as insignificant as an undergarment may not appear noteworthy in the twenty-first century, it was the talk of the town in 1949.

Ted Tinling was a man whose life revolved around tennis. Tinling held roles in the tennis world such as umpire, master of ceremonies, and historian, but he is most remembered as a women's tennis fashion designer, one who was always looking to push the envelope. After successfully adding a touch of colour to Joy Gannon's dresses in 1947, he ran into trouble when Hazel Wightman, the founder of the Wightman cup, frowned upon the Tinling-designed outfit of Britain's Betty Hilton which also showed hints of colour. Eventually, Tinling's designs resulted in the Wimbledon committee making an 'all white' fashion decree for its most pristine of tournaments. But Tinling was not a man who took the word 'no' for an answer, and when the Californian Gertrude 'Gussy' Moran came to Ted looking for an outfit with a little bit of an edge, Tinling had just the thing in mind.

And then it happened...Gorgeous Gussy, as she would soon come to be known, walked onto Centre Court wearing a short skirt and lace-trimmed undies that could be seen when Moran moved just so. Spectators tittered at the outfit, and before the umpire could say 'play', men strained for a glimpse and photographers lay on the ground to get the best angle of the sensation from Santa Monica. Although Gussy Moran didn't win the tournament, she made all the headlines. The infamous lace attire were even a topic for debate in parliament. And incredibly, Gorgeous Gussy didn't even have a website. Take that, Anna Kournikova.

The Tantrum

Jeff Tarango v. Alexander Mronz

Tennis's 79th most incredible moment occurred on 1 July 1995 at Wimbledon. The central character was the gritty 26-year-old left-handed American Jeff Tarango. On the one hand, Tarango was regarded as a talented player and a fierce competitor, but on the flip-side he was also known to be a volatile combatant who could fly off the handle at any moment. And Tarango was about to fully live up to his reputation...and then some. It was a seemingly benign third-round match on one of Wimbledon's outer courts. Tarango was in the middle of a highly competitive match with Germany's Alexander Mronz. With Mronz up a set and leading in the second, well-known umpire Bruno Rebeuh overruled a call. Tarango, who was displeased with the overrule, questioned Rebeuh's decision. Then things started getting ugly. Several members of the crowd began to boo and yell at Tarango. Tarango, who was never accused of being a master of diplomacy, told the crowd to 'shut up!' Rebeuh responded by slapping Tarango with a warning for an 'audible obscenity'. Tarango responded in his own right by calling Rebeuh 'corrupt'. Rebeuh shot back by assessing a point penalty against Tarango, costing him the game. After a supervisor stood by Rebeuh's decision, Tarango lost it.

And then it happened... Tarango stormed off the court to become the first player in the history of the Wimbledon Championships to default a match in progress for a reason not of a physical nature. But the drama wasn't over yet. After the match, Tarango's wife, Benedicte, tracked down Rebeuh and slapped him across the face to 'teach him a lesson'. And still, Tarango wasn't finished. In the press conference that followed the match, Tarango continually lambasted Rebeuh with allegations that he was 'the most corrupt official in the game'. When it was finally all said and done, Tarango was fined $63,576 for his antics. And although the fine was eventually reduced to $28,256 (his 1995 Wimbledon prize money), Tarango was barred from competing in Wimbledon the following year.

Jeff Tarango accomplished some commendable things in his professional career. He won two singles and 14 doubles titles, and earned more than three and a half million dollars (2,155,000 pounds) in prize money. But thanks to those infamous antics, Jeff Tarango will always be remembered first and foremost as the man who walked out on Wimbledon.

Do You Have Any Last Words?

Earl Cochell v. Gardner Mulloy

Tennis's 78th most incredible moment occurred at the 1951 US Championships. Earl Cochell was born on 18 May 1922 in Sacramento, California. Cochell had a very respectable amateur career with several year-end rankings in the top ten. In 1951, the 29-year-old was having another solid top ten year and had advanced to the fourth round at the US Championships. Cochell's opponent that day was Gardnar Mulloy, and neither Mulloy nor the Forest Hills crowd could have predicted what Cochell had in store for them. Apparently Cochell had awoken on the proverbial wrong side of the bed. Throughout the match Cochell was in an ornery mood. When he wasn't yelling at the linesmen, he was vehemently arguing with the referee, Ellsworth Davenport, and basically acting like an all-round moron. Eventually the New York crowd had had enough, and they let Cochell know it by booing and hissing their disapproval. At this point, Cochell tried to climb up the ladder into the chair umpire's seat to grab the microphone in an apparent attempt to give the crowd a few choice words of his own. And as if things weren't bad enough, Cochell started throwing in the towel at America's most prestigious tournament. That's right, he was losing the match on purpose. First he started playing left-handed, which wouldn't have been a big deal except for the fact that he was a righty. Cochell followed that up by serving, are you ready for this...underhand!

I guess it wouldn't be a real shocker to hear that Cochell lost that match 4-6, 6-2, 6-1, 6-2. But the story of this infamous day isn't over yet. Two days after the match the United States Lawn Tennis Association Executive Committee met to discuss a fair reprimand.

And then it happened...the distinguished members of the executive committee, in an unprecedented decision, voted to ban Cochell from tennis *for life*! Eventually the harsh ban was lifted, but not before the irreparable damage was done. Cochell would never again regain his old form and would forevermore be labelled with the distinction of being the only man or woman to receive the ultimate tennis punishment...The Lifetime Ban!

Pennies From Heaven

Adriano Panatta v. Bjorn Borg

Tennis's 77th most incredible moment occurred in 1978. Adriano Panatta was arguably the best player to come out of Italy in the Open Era. Born in Rome on 9 July 1950, Panatta had the looks to make women swoon and a game to match. He used his big serve and athletic volleying to win five career titles, ultimately achieving a ranking that topped out at number seven in the world in 1976. Although Panatta was successful on several surfaces, he was always most at home on the slow red clay courts that were indigenous to his homeland of Italy. It would come on just such a surface that Adriano would make his biggest marks on the game he loved. Not only did Panatta lead his country to its only Davis Cup title on the slow, gruelling surface in 1976, but he also won his only major title on the red earth of the French Open in that same year when he defeated Guillermo Vilas in the finals.

Not surprisingly, the incredible moment involving Adriano Panatta and Bjorn Borg came on clay. The setting was the 1978 Italian Open and the favourite, and number one seed, Bjorn Borg was cruising through the top side of the draw. The surprise was coming on the bottom half where the unseeded hometown favourite, Panatta, had upset second-seeded Vitas Gerulaitis in the first round and, bolstered by the partisan Italian crowd, continued to roll. After the semi-final matches in which Borg defeated Eddie Dibbs in straight sets and Jose Higueras had to retire against Panatta, the Italian dream final was set to go. It matched the world's premier clay court player against Italy's favourite son.

The match got underway without incident, with Panatta winning the first set, 6-1 and Borg taking the second, 6-3.

And then it happened... It's hard to say exactly when it started, but seemingly coins started to fall from the sky onto Borg's side of the court, or more specifically on his head! Soon it became clear that the crazed Italian fans were actually tossing coins at the Swedish champion in an attempt to throw the favourite off of his game. But as would be Bjorn's MO throughout his storied career, he would not be distracted nor deterred. In fact, the classy Borg would simply pick up the coins and put them in his pocket. And in case that didn't infuriate the Panatta fans enough, Borg would obtain the ultimate revenge by defeating Panatta in five sets by the score of 1-6, 6-3, 6-1, 4-6, 6-3 to take the match and the title. At the end of the day, it appeared that Borg not only took home the winner's paycheque, but got a few extra lira for his efforts as well.

No Pain No Gain

Shuzo Matsuoka v. Petr Korda

Tennis's 76th most incredible moment occurred during the 1995 US Open. The Open, as it is proudly referred to by Americans, has long been heralded as the toughest two weeks in tennis – more difficult than the other three Grand Slam events. The crowds are bigger, louder, and – how can I say this politely – more raucous than your average fans. To put it bluntly, they're New Yorkers. And although New York might be an ideal setting to play a baseball or American football game, the concentration and precision necessary to play top-notch tennis doesn't always lend itself to the nature of the boisterous Big Apple crowd. And don't get me started with the traffic, the crowds, the press... and if you've been paying attention you may have noticed that I haven't even mentioned the minute fact that one has to win seven best-of-five-set matches in a two-week period to capture the title. To put it mildly, a daunting task. But, on the plus side, it makes for some damn exciting tennis!

This brings us to the little-known Japanese player named Shuzo Matsuoka. Matsuoka was born in Tokyo on 6 November 1967. Although his career may not go down as a footnote in the annals of tennis history (his match record was 147 wins and 163 losses), he did win one title in Seoul and reached the quarter-finals of Wimbledon in 1995. But just a couple of months after his breakout Grand Slam performance on grass,

Matsuoka was poised to keep the momentum rolling at the US Open. As fate would have it, Shuzo's first round opponent was the formidable Czech Petr Korda. Despite the fact that Korda was the favourite, many analysts were picking the Matsuoka-Korda match-up as one to watch. And what a match it turned out to be! Staged under the hot sun, the two gladiators battled feverishly, and after hours of playing their guts out they found themselves all tied up at two sets apiece. As the fifth and deciding set got underway, both men were exhausted. But neither gave an inch.

And then it happened...under the glaring sun, Matsuoka began to cramp. And as the match continued the Japanese player's cramps got worse and worse until Shuzo was lying down on the court, writhing in pain. Yet, unbelievably, no one could come to his aid. You see, in 1995, the official rules stated that a player who was cramping was not entitled to an injury time-out because it was considered a lack of conditioning, as opposed to an unforeseen injury sustained during play. As Matsuoka continued to lie helplessly on the court, the crowd, the officials, the trainers and even Korda could do nothing but stand by idly and watch the ghastly scene. Finally, after what seemed like an eternity, Matsuoka declared that he could no longer continue and consequently forfeited the match in order to receive medical care. The good news is that, largely as a result of the 'Matsuoka incident', the rule was finally changed, thus allowing cramping players to receive medical assistance without being forced to forfeit. But during that now infamous first-round match, it was Matsuoka's 'no pain-no gain' attitude that resulted in tennis's 76th most incredible moment.

The Battle Down Under

Andy Roddick v. Younes El Aynaoui

Tennis's 75th most incredible moment occurred at the 2003 Australian Open. When John McEnroe and Jimmy Connors were coming to the end of their illustrious Hall of Fame careers, the American tennis community was asking the same nervous question: 'Where is the next great crop of American players?' Well, sure enough a few guys by the name of Sampras, Agassi, Courier and Chang took the gauntlet and ran with it. And as this group of American idols rode off into the sunset, the American tennis community was once again asking, 'Who's next?'

Enter Andy Roddick, who was quickly climbing the tennis ladder and ended the 2002 season ranked as one of the world's top players. Yet despite his impressive results, many impatient tennis fans were quick to point out that Roddick had failed to make a breakthrough in one of the Grand Slam tournaments. Although Roddick had reached the US Open quarter-finals twice, he had yet to reach a final four. But as the 2003 season began, many tennis enthusiasts were hopeful that this would be Andy's first big year. As the year's first Grand Slam, the Australian Open, got underway, Roddick was playing well and found himself in the fourth round against the Russian Mikhail Youzhney. Youzhney, who was the hero in Russia's upset victory over France in the 2002 Davis Cup final, was leading Roddick by two sets to love and appeared well on his way to the quarter-finals. But Roddick, who has already distinguished himself as a player with a lion's heart, roared back to take the match in five sets.

When players come off a gruelling match, they always hope for an easy contest the next round. And when Roddick faced Younes El Aynaoui of Morocco in the quarter-finals, the physically and mentally exhausted Roddick must have been praying for an easy straight-sets victory. But lo and behold, the tennis gods and Younes El Aynaoui had something else in store for him.

As the night-time match got underway, both men had aspirations of making it to their first ever Grand Slam semi-final appearance. Initially, things looked good for the Moroccan when he took the first set 6-4. Yet Roddick, with his champion's resolve, fought back to even the match by taking the second-set tiebreaker, 7 points to 5. When El Aynaoui took the third set 6-4, Roddick knew that if he wanted to advance he would have to win his second straight five-set match. Undeterred, Roddick won the fourth set 6-4, setting the stage for the conclusion to the most important match at the time in the lives of these two warriors.

And then it happened...as the fifth set wore on, neither man would give an inch. El Aynaoui had the first real chance when he held a match point with Roddick serving at 4-5. But when Roddick unleashed an enormous inside out forehand winner, El Aynaoui's hopes vanished and Roddick went on to hold serve. With no fifth-set tiebreaker at the Australian Open, the two physically spent players had no choice but to continue to fight with their minds and their hearts. The duel went on until Roddick finally got a chance when he broke El Aynaoui's serve to go ahead 11-10. But El Aynaoui, who was now fighting cramps, battled back to break Roddick and even the match at 11 games all. And on and on they went. Fifteen all, 16 all, 17 all...until finally, mercifully, Roddick served out the match to win the longest final set, to that date, in Grand Slam history, 21-19, in a match that lasted four hours and 59 minutes. As the two men hugged at the net and took a bow together in front of a well-deserved standing ovation, television analyst Mary Carrillo stated that it had been a distinct honour and a privilege to be a witness to this contest. Mary, I couldn't have said it better myself.

But as all tennis fans are well aware, the Roddick–El Aynaoui final set would eventually pale in comparison to what was to come at Wimbledon in 2010. (See Incredible Bonus Moment #3.)

The King of Clay

Rafael Nadal

Tennis's 74th most incredible moment occurred between April 2005 and May 2007 (as I stated previously...some moments are longer than others). Rafael Nadal was born on 3 June 1986 in Manacor, Majorca. As a young boy little 'Rafa' excelled as an athlete in both football and tennis. However, when he reached age 12 his father, concerned that his school work would suffer, made his son choose between the two sports. Nadal decided upon tennis and it would be a decision that would change the history of our great sport.

As the young tennis prodigy developed, it quickly became clear that he had the potential for greatness. This was never more apparent than when he was playing on clay, Spain's ubiquitous tennis surface. For example, in May 2001, the 14-year-old Nadal defeated Pat Cash, the 1986 Wimbledon Champion (see incredible moment #65), in a clay court exhibition. And at the tender age of 16, he was already ranked in the world's top 50.

Two years later, in April of 2005, Rafael he won a seemingly insignificant first-round clay court match. This led to another clay court win, and then another, and another. As the victories began to mount, so did the hype. With the tennis world watching every stroke, Nadal defeated Robin Soderling in the first round of the 2006 French Open, and in doing so he broke Guillermo Vilas' 29-year-old record clay court winning streak of 53 consecutive matches. (Ironically Soderling would avenge this loss by upsetting Nadal in the 2009 French Open abruptly ending his bid for 5 straight French Open titles – see incredible moment #7). But he didn't stop there. Rafael later surpassed the legendary John McEnroe's consecutive same-surface winning streak of 75 matches. (McEnroe achieved the feat on indoor carpet.)

As the streak continued to an incredible 81 consecutive clay court victories, Nadal found himself in the finals of the Hamburg Masters tournament to face his rival and world's number one, the great Roger Federer. Federer had not won a title in his last four tournaments, his longest dry spell since he became number one in February 2004.

He was also 0-5 lifetime against Nadal on clay, but he had won this tournament three times in the past and was considered by many to be the one man who had a legitimate chance to knock off Rafa, the Clay Court King.

As the finals got underway it looked like it was going to be more of the same as Rafael won the first set handily, 6-2. But Roger Federer wasn't considered the best all-round player in the world for nothing, and he fought back to take the second set by the same score, 6-2. And incredibly, as a stunned German crowd looked on, Federer continued to roll. He took a commanding five-game-to-love final set lead...

And then it happened...Federer put away a final winning shot, thus ending Nadal's awesome record at 81 straight matches. During the streak, Rafael won an incredible 13 straight clay court titles, including two French Opens. And just in case you find yourself feeling sorry for the then 20-year-old Majorcan, a couple of weeks later he got his revenge as he defeated – you guessed it – Roger Federer in the French Open finals for the third straight time.

I Scream, You Scream, We All Scream - For Ice Cream?

Tony Pickard v. Ian Crookenden

Tennis's 73rd most incredible moment occurred at the 1963 Italian Championships. This incredible moment involved the Englishman Tony Pickard, who had devoted most of his life to tennis. From a tennis professional and a Davis Cup member, Pickard went on to become a Davis Cup captain and a successful coach for the likes of Stefan Edberg and Greg Rusedski. Pickard has probably seen all that tennis has to offer in his lifetime involvement around the sport. But it was in a match at the 1963 Italian Championships in Rome against the New Zealander Ian Crookenden that caused even the most seasoned tennis fans to stand up and take notice. It was a very hot day and the match was a lengthy one. Pickard was leading Crookenden two sets to one and had finally reached match point in the fourth set.

And then it happened...Crookenden hit a shot that was said to be at least nine inches over the baseline. Game, set and match Pickard...right? Well, not so fast. There was no call of 'out'. As the players, the chair umpire and the crowd looked to the linesman for the call it became evident why the linesman remained silent. An ice-cream vendor had been walking right behind the court and apparently the players were not the only ones who had become over-heated during the long, gruelling match. As the ball was being hit long, the linesman was apparently buying an ice-cream over the fence. And believe it or not, in those days the players were not allowed to appeal calls. There was nothing Pickard could do except to play on. And as often happens in sports, the tide turned on the one crucial missed call and before Pickard could say 'blimey', Crookenden had come back to win the match in five sets.

Now that's what I'd call one costly ice-cream cone.

Now That's What I Call Stingy

Suzanne Lenglen

Tennis's 72nd most incredible moment occurred at the 1925 Wimbledon Championships. Suzanne Rachel Flore Lenglen was born on 24 May 1899 in Campiegne, France. And it appeared as if Suzanne's father Charles had a master plan for his daughter from the time she was an infant. Suzanne was groomed to be the greatest tennis champion of her generation...and that's exactly what happened. But it didn't come without a lot of hard work and anguish. Charles, who was known to be a taskmaster, would keep Suzanne out on the courts for hours at a time. If Suzanne had a poor practice session her father would deny her jam for her bread, and when she performed well he would treat her like the family pet, rewarding her with brandy-soaked sugar cubes. Not that I'm condoning such behaviour, but in this case it sure seemed to work.

Suzanne's greatness was never more apparent than on the grass courts of Wimbledon, for Lenglen was ahead of her time in many aspects. Whether it was her tennis attire, which scandalously exposed her calves and forearms, or her attacking style of play, La Grande Suzanne was definitely a trend setter. Yet it was Suzanne's never before seen aggressive all court style of play which made her game most suited for the Big 'W'. Incredibly, Lenglen won the Wimbledon singles and doubles titles five years in a row from 1919 through 1923. And after the streak ended when Lenglen was forced to withdraw from the tournament in 1924 due to illness, she was ready to come back with a vengeance in 1925. In fact it seemed as if all of France was ready to conquer The Championships of Wimbledon that particular year. The French players took the men's singles and doubles titles, the women's singles and half of the women's doubles title (Lenglen teamed up with American Elizabeth Ryan), and the mixed doubles title as well.

Yet history was really made when Lenglen displayed her arsenal in a way that the Wimbledon fortnight has never seen, before or since. After destroying opponent after opponent for the first three rounds of the then five-round tournament, Lenglen overwhelmed Kitty McKane 6-0, 6-0 in the semi-finals. Incredibly, through her first four matches, Lenglen had only lost three games as she prepared to face Joan Fry of England for the title.

And then it happened...Lenglen once again overpowered and outclassed her foe by winning 6-2, 6-0. Lenglen had prevailed as a Wimbledon champion for the sixth time and unbelievably lost only five... that's right, five measly games during the entire tournament! Unfortunately, at the 1926 Wimbledon tournament, Lenglen found herself in hot water when she was tardy for a match in front of King George V and Queen Mary. The controversy was too much for the emotionally fragile Lenglen and she subsequently turned professional, thus ending a spectacular amateur career.

You Cannot Be Serious!

John McEnroe v. Tom Gullickson

Tennis's 71st most incredible moment occurred during a first-round match at Wimbledon in 1981. A first-round match you ask? What kind of incredible moment could occur during a seemingly insignificant first-round match? Well, John McEnroe was involved...does that help answer some of the questions? Johnny Mac was playing the future US Davis Cup Captain Tom Gullickson when John's serve kicked up chalk. When the serve was called out, an unhappy McEnroe went up to the chair umpire, Edward James, to 'discuss' the matter, pointing out that 'chalk flew up!' James explained that there was some excess chalk that was scattered slightly behind the service line and that accounted for the dust that McEnroe saw airborne. But the 22-year-old McEnroe, who was quoted as saying, 'I know I can see the ball better than the officials' wasn't going to accept that explanation. At that point McEnroe, let's just say...went berserk.

And then it happened...Mac uttered the phrase that would go down in tennis history. 'You cannot be serious!' he shouted. (These words would even grace the title of his 2002 bestselling autobiography.) But the 'Superbrat', as he was dubbed by the tabloids, wasn't finished. After receiving a warning, he was given a point penalty when he told James, 'You're the pits of the world.' And even when McEnroe demanded to see the referee because he was not going to let 'an incompetent fool' deduct a point, it was to no avail. Incredibly, after the tantrum McEnroe was able to compose himself, as he usually seemed to do, and went on to win the match. In fact, McEnroe made his way to the final where he showed uncharacteristically good behaviour in defeating the five-time defending champion Bjorn Borg to win his first of three Wimbledon titles. When all was said and done, the talented Mr. McEnroe would add four US Open Championships to his three Wimbledon titles. Furthermore, he had one of the best Davis Cup records of all time, and would end the year ranked as the number one player in the world a total of four times. Yet despite his great talent and tennis accomplishments, John McEnroe will always be remembered as much for his tantrums as for his titles. And due to a service call that many players would have probably overlooked, John McEnroe uttered those infamous words that will always be a part of tennis history.

Bravo Manolo

Manuel Orantes

Tennis's 70th most incredible moment occurred at the 1975 US Open. Manuel 'Manolo' Orantes was born on 6 February 1949. A cagey left-hander from Granada, Spain, Orantes had a career which saw him win 32 singles titles and hold a top ten ranking between 1975 and 1977. But by far the pinnacle of Orantes' career came at the 1975 US Open. The Open, which was staged at Forest Hills, had previously been played on grass. However, in 1975 the surface was switched to a slow Har-Tru court to the delight of the natural baseliners from South America and Europe. Orantes was just such a player, and he took full advantage of being seeded number 3 by fighting his way all the way to the semi-finals. His opponent in the final four was a man equally adept on clay. That man was the second-seeded Guillermo Vilas of Argentina. The 1975 US Open was the tournament where night play was ushered in to Grand Slam tennis. And this semi-final match-up between Orantes and Vilas proved that tennis under the lights was a welcome addition to the US Open.

The match began at approximately 7 pm on a Saturday. Orantes lost the first set 6-4 and Vilas kept the pressure on by taking the second set 6-1. When Vilas grabbed an early break in the third and went up 2-0, it couldn't have looked bleaker for Orantes. And although Manolo fought back gallantly to win the third set 6-2, it looked like curtains for sure when he fell behind 5-0 and faced three match points.

And then it happened... Orantes kept fighting and won the game, but the reprieve was short-lived and in the very next game Vilas held two more match points. Unbelievably, Orantes battled back to win that game as well. With Vilas most likely thinking about missed opportunities, Orantes went on a roll. And in one of the greatest comebacks in Grand Slam history, Orantes went on to win the set and the match 4-6, 1-6, 6-2, 7-5, 6-4. The three hour and 44 minute struggle didn't end until 10:40 pm, after which Orantes rushed home to get a good night's sleep before facing the top-seeded Jimmy Connors in the finals. Unfortunately, the overnight events could only come under the umbrella of 'Murphy's Law'. Due to a plumbing problem in his hotel room, Orantes didn't get to bed until 3 am! Yet it appeared that the tennis gods were on his side because he pulled off the upset in shocking fashion by easily dismissing Connors, 6-4, 6-3, 6-3.

Ten years had passed since Manuel Santana became the first Spaniard to win the US title and now Spain could cheer again as one of their own claimed the title. Bravo, Manolo, Bravo!

Chrissie America

Chris Evert v. Martina Navratilova

Tennis's 69th most incredible moment occurred at the French Open final in 1985. Martina Navratilova and Chris Evert (then Chris Evert Lloyd) enjoyed one of the greatest rivalries in all of sports. They played 80 times, generally in the finals of tournaments, between the years of 1973 and 1988. And while Chris dominated the first half of their rivalry, Martina had her way through the later years. By the time the two combatants met in the final of the 1985 French Open, Navratilova had prevailed in 15 of their previous 16 match-ups. And her confidence was further bolstered by the fact that Navratilova had thrashed Evert Lloyd in the finals of the 1984 French Open by the score of 6-3, 6-1. Yet on the day of the 1985 final Evert Lloyd was aided by a plan that she and her husband John Lloyd (with whom she was separated but still friendly) had devised before the match.

John, a tennis professional in his own right, had advised Chris to hit high-bouncing topspin balls to Navratilova's forehand to hinder her ability to hit slice approach shots and get to the net where she felt most comfortable. As the match got underway on a very windy day in Paris, the plan was working beautifully. Evert Lloyd jumped out to a three games to love lead. And even though Martina fought back to three games all, Chris's best shot, her two-fisted backhand, was sharper than usual, and she used it to help her win the next three games and secure the first set,

6-3. Evert Lloyd continued to ride her backhand and her momentum into the second set to take a commanding 4-2 lead. In the seventh game she held game points for 5-2, but at this point Navratilova dug in and pushed the set to a tiebreaker, which she won seven points to four.

In the deciding set Evert Lloyd jumped ahead 3-1 before Navratilova fought back to even the score at three all. Again Evert Lloyd prevailed, taking the next two games, but Navratilova recovered once more to level the match, this time at 5 games all. The suspense of the seesaw match was overwhelming. Then, when Martina jumped out to a love-40 lead on Chris's serve, it seemed as if the Czech-turned-American Navratilova had finally taken control of the match. But Chris Evert Lloyd, America's sweetheart, fought back and held serve. Now with Martina serving to stay alive once again, she could tempt fate no longer.

And then it happened...as Evert Lloyd reached match point she hit one more of her patented backhand passing shots, and in doing so won her sixth French Open Championship! Of all the great matches played in their historic rivalry, this is considered to be the crème de la crème, the greatest match of them all. A disappointed but gracious Navratilova was able to acknowledge the high quality of the contest. Afterwards, she called it 'one of the most incredible matches you can ever imagine. It had everything.' It sure did!

Giant Killer

Boris Becker v. Derrick Rostagno

Tennis's 68th-most incredible moment occurred at the 1989 US Open. Derrick Rostagno was born on 25 October 1965 in Hollywood, California. In his tennis career, Rostagno had a so-so record of 191 wins to 184 losses. Derrick did manage to capture an ATP title in New Haven, Connecticut in 1990, but he will always be remembered first and foremost as a tour giant killer. Although his results were somewhat inconsistent, he periodically could knock off a top player on any given day. Consequently, whenever a highly ranked player was to face Derrick, he knew that he had to be at his best, or else risk defeat.

At the 1989 US Open, when the highly regarded Boris Becker was to face Rostagno in the second round, Boris must have been ready for a fight. For not only was Becker well aware of Rostagno's reputation, but just one year earlier Derrick had advanced all the way to the 1988 US Open quarter-finals. As the match got underway, it looked like Rostagno was wielding his magic once again. Before the German knew what hit him, the handsome, 6′ 3″ California boy had swiped the first set with apparent ease, six games to one. And although the second set was tighter, the ultimate outcome was the same; Rostagno took it in a tiebreaker seven points to one for a commanding two sets to love advantage. But with his back against the wall, Boris came out swinging and took the third set 6-3. The fourth set proved to be nip and tuck with both men scraping and clawing with everything they had. Eventually, the set would be decided by a tiebreaker. Becker was trying to push the match into a fifth set whereas Rostagno was vying to carve out another huge upset victory notch on his belt. When Rostagno took a six points to four advantage he held two match points. Becker then summoned up his courage and fought off the first. On the second match point Rostagno decided to take it to the three-time Wimbledon champion by charging the net. Becker chased down the approach and unleashed a forehand passing shot, but Derrick was there waiting, poised to put the volley into the open court and claim victory.

And then it happened…the tennis gods must have been in Boris's corner because his passing shot clipped the net cord, hopped over Rostagno's racquet, and fell within the lines. Point Becker! As the crowd let out a gasp, the shell-shocked Rostagno lost the next two points, the tiebreaker and the set. Rostagno never recovered from that twist of fate as Becker cruised through the fifth to take the match 1-6, 6-7, 6-3, 7-6, 6-3. Ultimately 'Boom-Boom' took advantage of his good fortune to make his way to the finals and then defeated the perennial US Open finalist Ivan Lendl in four heavy-hitting sets.

Rostagno, the giant killer, had probably come to believe 'the bigger they are, the harder they fall'. Unfortunately for Derrick, this giant fell smack on top of him.

The Fourth Musketeer

Yannick Noah

Tennis's 67th most incredible moment occurred at the 1983 French Open. Yannick Simone Camille Noah was born on 18 May 1960 to a French mother and a Cameroonian father. In 1971, while playing tennis on the courts of Cameroon, young Yannick received a one in a million opportunity when American star Arthur Ashe noticed his talent. Ashe suggested that the French Tennis Federation take a look at the 11-year-old prodigy. In short order, a very young Yannick left his family and moved to France, and in a few years, when the 6' 4", 190-pound (86-kilo) Noah grew into his game, he was ready for the pro circuit. Throughout his first few years on the tour Yannick methodically moved up the rankings until he finally broke into the top ten in 1982. Yet despite his early success at the time of the 1983 French Open, the 23-year-old Noah had not been able to advance past the quarter-finals of a Grand Slam event. But this time, at his country's tennis crown jewel tournament, things would prove to be different. From the first round, Noah's attacking serve and volley style was somehow successful against the odds on the ultra slow French clay.

Although Noah tore through the first four matches without losing a set, many thought his Grand Slam adventure would once again end in the quarter-finals when his opponent was the clay court standout, Ivan Lendl. Although Lendl would eventually become a three-time French Open champion, this year would be Yannick's turn to shine as he defeated Ivan in four sets. Noah's next opponent was the surprise of the tournament. Christophe Roger-Vasselin came into the French Open ranked 230th in the world. But when he shocked the tennis establishment by upsetting top-seeded Jimmy Connors in straight sets, it set up an all-French semi-final match-up. After Noah easily disposed of Roger-Vasselin 6-3, 6-0, 6-0, he was poised to become the first Frenchman to win his country's singles title since Marcel Bernard did so 37 years earlier.

Waiting for Yannick in the finals was defending champion Mats Wilander of Sweden. Although Wilander was the consensus favourite, Noah, spurred on by the partisan Parisian crowd, took the first set 6-2. When Noah continued his fine play to claim the tight second set 7-5 it looked as if the unthinkable might occur. As the third set went to a tiebreaker the crowd held its collective breath. Noah took a six points to three advantage and held triple championship point.

And then it happened...Yannick Noah took one final mighty service swat, and when Wilander's return sailed over the baseline it was over. Game, set and championship, Noah! The crowd erupted and Noah burst into tears as he hugged his father. Noah had done what was seemingly inconceivable just two weeks earlier. He had won the French Open and in doing so wrote a piece of tennis history.

Brotherly Love

William Renshaw

Tennis's 66th most incredible moment occurred in 1886. William Charles Renshaw was born in Leamington on 3 January 1861. Known to all as Willie, Renshaw and his twin brother Ernest were two of the greatest players in the game's infancy. The two twins played an aggressive game for that era. Yet it would be younger brother (by 15 minutes) Willie who would become one of the greatest Wimbledon Champions of all time. It all started in 1880 when Willie played in his first Wimbledon. After winning his first two matches, Renshaw lost to O.E. Woodhouse in the third round. But as history would prove, Renshaw would not lose again at Wimbledon for *six years*! The streak began in 1881 when Willie captured his first Wimbledon title by lambasting two-time defending champion John Hartley in the finals 6-0, 6-2, 6-1. Willie would follow up his 1881 victory by defeating his brother Ernest in the finals in 1882 and 1883, both times in five sets. Renshaw would then go on to win his fourth straight title in 1884 by defeating Herbert Lawford in straight sets and followed that up by conquering Lawford again for his fifth consecutive title, this time in four hard fought sets.

In the 1886 finals, Renshaw was to face Lawford for the third straight time. As the combatants began to play it appeared as if it was going to be more of the same for poor Herbert Lawford as Willie won the first set six games to love. But Lawford was not going to go down without a fight and came back to win the second set 7-5. Renshaw then won the third set 6-3 and went ahead 5-4 in the fourth.

And then it happened...Renshaw captured the final game to win his sixth straight men's Wimbledon title, a record that has yet to be matched. Unfortunately, Renshaw was unable to defend his title in 1887 due to an elbow injury. After losing in the quarter-finals in 1888, he went on to win his seventh and last Wimbledon singles championship in 1889 by defeating his brother in the finals once again. And if it seems that the younger twin stole all the thunder, it turned out that Willie wasn't such a bad brother after all. Willie teamed up with his brother Ernest to win seven Wimbledon doubles titles between 1880 and 1889. Consequently, in the tennis world the 1880s became known as 'The Renshaw Rush'. Now that's what I call brotherly love.

Cash Is Better Than a Czech

Pat Cash v. Ivan Lendl

Tennis's 65th most incredible moment occurred in the 1987 Wimbledon final. The participants were the world's number one, Ivan Lendl, versus the Australian number one, Pat Cash. Lendl, who would end his career with eight Grand Slam titles, was desperately looking for the one major which continually eluded him, Wimbledon. For his part, the young 22-year-old Cash was trying to secure the first of what he hoped would be many Grand Slam titles to follow. Furthermore, both men were trying to overcome all too recent painful memories. Cash had lost in the final of his home country's championship, the Australian Open, six months earlier; Lendl was beaten in the Wimbledon final one year earlier by a German you may have heard of by the name of Boris 'Boom Boom' Becker.

As the finals got underway it soon became clear that the flamboyant, check-headband-wearing Pat Cash was the crowd favourite over the dour Czech-turned-American. Cash thrilled the partisan crowd by squeaking out a first set tiebreaker seven points to five. As Cash continued to play near-perfect grass court tennis, he seemed to be on cruise control as he won the second set 6-2. And despite the fact that Lendl, the hardest working player in tennis, continued to fight to the end, it was all for naught as Cash won the title in straight sets, 7-5 in the third. Pat Cash had done it! He had won his first Grand Slam title and it was none other than the granddaddy of them all, Wimbledon.

And then it happened...with the crowd cheering its approval, the new champion couldn't wait to celebrate with his family and friends. Instead of receiving the customary kudos from the Duke and Duchess of Kent, the spontaneous Cash climbed into the crowd in an attempt to celebrate with his loved ones in the friends' box. Unfortunately, or comically as it turned out, Cash hadn't prudently planned his journey to the second tier of Centre Court and the champion took several wrong turns before finally arriving at his intended destination. As Cash received hugs and kisses from his entourage, a feel-good atmosphere permeated the crowd and the TV viewing public. Unknowingly, Cash became a trendsetter. Nowadays it appears that rarely an opportunity passes when a victorious player doesn't run to share the moment with his or her family at courtside. But lest we forget, it was Pat Cash who was the first to celebrate in such a fashion. Cash never did win another Grand Slam championship, and Ivan Lendl never did win that elusive Wimbledon title. But as a sign in the stands stated so eloquently on that history making July day, Cash was certainly better than a Czech.

I Didn't Get the Point

Hazel Hotchkiss v. Miss Huiskamp

Tennis's 64th most incredible moment occurred in 1910. Hazel Virginia Hotchkiss was born in 1886. A Californian, Hotchkiss was one of the first women to use the volley consistently in her attacking game. Ms Hotchkiss, who died in 1974, is remembered by tennis historians for many accomplishments. She won US Singles titles in 1909–1911 and again in 1919, ultimately capturing a total of 17 major singles and doubles titles. And after marrying George Wightman in 1912 she eventually envisioned the Wightman tournament as a women's alternative to the men's Davis Cup. Obviously, Hotchkiss, who was inducted into the International Tennis Hall of Fame, has contributed many memorable moments to the history of tennis. Yet tennis's 64th most incredible moment was one that no one saw coming.

In tennis, as in all competitive sports, the objective is to defeat your opponent. And although a sense of noble fulfilment can come from spurring each other to higher and higher levels of competition, there is an almost perverse satisfaction in destroying one's adversary. To dominate from beginning to end, and leave no doubt that you are the better player, is the name of the game in professional sports. On very rare occasion a player is so dominant that he or she wins a set without losing a single point. This feat has been coined a 'golden set'. Yet there is no universal term for winning a match without losing a point, for the single reason that it almost never happens. The key word here is 'almost'.

In the prime of her career, Ms Hotchkiss was playing in a seemingly insignificant tournament in Seattle in 1910. When a player known only by the name of Miss Huiskamp stepped onto the court to face Hotchkiss, almost everybody gave her little chance of winning the match. And they would soon find out how right they were. As the match got underway, Hotchkiss got off to a fast start, winning the first game at love. As the players switched sides again, Hotchkiss was now up three love and was still yet to relinquish a point. And in what seemed to be the time it takes to say 'golden set', Hotchkiss had won the first set without losing a point. Unfortunately for Huiskamp the second set was more of the same. As Hotchkiss hit winner after winner and Huiskamp made error after error, the contest mercifully came to match point.

And then it happened...Hotchkiss struck the final blow and became the only player in the history of big-time tennis to notch a win without losing a single point. Two golden sets in a perfect match. Now that's what I call a good day at the office.

Nobody's Perfect

Kathy Horvath v. Martina Navratilova

Tennis's 63rd incredible moment occurred on 28 May 1983 at the French Open. It involved a fourth-round match-up between the world's number one player Martina Navratilova and the American teenager Kathy Horvath. Navratilova had been dominating the women's tour for the first part of the 1983 season to the tune of a 36-0 record. It appeared as if no woman could stop the most talented, hardworking player in the game, playing at the pinnacle of her career...especially the little-known, unseeded Horvath. And although Horvath had reached the finals of the German Open, a French Open tune-up tournament the previous week, no one in the tennis world gave her a snowball's chance in hell of even putting a scare into Martina...she was just that good. But as the match got underway, the unthinkable began to happen. Horvath was matching Martina shot for shot and when the first set was over Horvath had actually won, 6-4. But just as quickly as the upset rumours were spreading around Stade Roland Garros, Martina seemed to quash them. In a quick turnaround, Martina had taken back complete control of the match and won the second set 6-0.

And then it happened...Just as Navratilova was taking a deep breath, Horvath turned it up another notch and began playing some of the best tennis of her career. In the end, Horvath shocked Martina and the tennis world by taking the final set, 6-3. And as stunning as this upset was, it wasn't until the end of the year that the full ramifications of the Navratilova defeat were fully realised. After the loss to Horvath, Martina went on to win Wimbledon, the US Open and finally the Australian Open. As a matter of fact, Navratilova didn't lose another match for all of 1983. Horvath's stunning upset not only cost Martina the Grand Slam that year, but, as it turned out, upended what would have been the only perfect season in the Open Era. Horvath, who had been a child prodigy, would go on to win five tournaments in her career. But thanks to one shining moment, Kathy Horvath will always be remembered most for one of the most stunning and significant upsets in the history of the game.

Better to be Lucky Than Good

Ted Schroeder

Tennis's 62nd most incredible moment occurred at the Wimbledon Championships in 1949. Fredrick Rudolph 'Ted' Schroeder was one of the leading players of the 1940s. Born on 20 July 1921 in Newark, New Jersey, Schroeder was known for many things throughout his career. He was a top ten player for six straight years, an exceptional Davis Cup player, only the second player ever to win the US collegiate title and US championships in the same year, and even served in the US Naval Air Force during World War II. But 'Lucky Ted', as he would come to be known, will always be best remembered for his heroic efforts at Wimbledon in 1949.

In 1949 Schroeder was only a part-time player who would take breaks from his business career to play a little tennis, or in this case play for the most prestigious title in the game. In his first appearance at the Big 'W', Schroeder found immediate difficulty when he went down two sets to love to Gardnar Mulloy in the first round. But the top-seeded Schroeder fought back to take the next two sets and finally prevailed 7-5 in the fifth. After finding an easier time advancing through the next three matches 'Lucky Ted' would have to pull out his rabbit's foot once again in the quarter-finals, and this time he would need to rub it with all his might. Playing for a spot in the final four, Schroeder lost the first two sets once again 3-6, 6-8, but as would be his MO throughout the fortnight he continued to battle gallantly. After taking the next two sets 6-3, 6-2, he would face a match point at 4-5 in the final set. After a foot fault was called on his first serve Schroeder coolly put in his second and rushed the net. The return came back in a flash and Ted stuck out his racquet.

And then it happened...the volley glanced off Lucky Ted's frame and fell into the court for a mishit winner! Incredibly, Schroeder faced another match point at 5-6 and staved that one off with a backhand pass, eventually taking the match 9-7 in the decider. Ted would tempt fate again when he fell behind two sets to one in the semis but once again fought back for the victory. And in the championship match, you guessed it, he went five sets for the fourth time in his seven matches and came out on top yet again when he defeated Jaroslav Drobny for the title 3-6, 6-0, 6-3, 4-6, 6-4. Incredibly, in his only career Wimbledon appearance, Schroeder tempted fate and emerged unscathed to become a Wimbledon champion. But this great sport of ours is both fickle and humbling, and several months later in the US Championship final Schroeder was not so lucky when he let his two-set advantage slip away as he lost to Pancho Gonzalez in five sets.

Just Put Me on a Court, Any Court

Bjorn Borg

Tennis's 61st most incredible moment occurred between 1978 and 1980. Bjorn Borg was born on 6 June 1956 in Sodertalje, Sweden. Young Bjorn picked up the game when his father won a tennis racquet in a ping-pong tournament and gave it to his son as a gift. The future champion fell in love with the game immediately. And as every tennis fan is well aware, Bjorn Borg grew up to become one of the greatest tennis artists of all time. Yet one of his greatest accomplishments is often overlooked. Tennis players, like all athletes, have their areas of strength and weakness. There are some players who excel with their serves while others favour their backhand. Even the professionals have preferences. For example, certain players are more comfortable on court surfaces that most suit their games. An attacking serve-and-volleyer is normally happiest on a fast grass surface such as at Wimbledon, while a defensive baseliner is most often at his best on a slow clay court typified by the French Open. Consequently, even the best of the best typically do well at the same tournaments while they continually fail at others. Attackers such as Becker, Sampras and McEnroe won multiple Wimbledon titles but never succeeded at the French. Conversely, great baseliners such as Lendl, Rosewall and Sanchez Vicario had great success at the French but failed to win Wimbledon. Not only are there no two tennis surfaces with less in common than the French

Open and Wimbledon, but to make things even more difficult they occur only two weeks apart. The adjustment from clay to grass in a short time period makes the task of winning both major titles in the same year daunting to say the least.

Despite these formidable challenges, the great Bjorn Borg had already captured French Open titles in 1974 and 1975, and Wimbledon victories in 1976 and 1977. Now he was poised to make history in 1978. After defeating Guillermo Vilas in straight sets in the 1978 French final, Bjorn was off to play once more on the British grass. Incredibly, he pulled off the rare 'European double' by defeating Connors in straight sets for his third straight Wimbledon crown.

But the Swedish heartthrob was not done...not even close. After winning his second straight French title in 1979 over Victor Pecci, and his fourth French title overall, it was off to the grass courts of the All-England Club where he pulled off the double again by defeating Roscoe Tanner in a five-set thriller for his fourth straight Wimbledon. And then, in 1980, after winning the French over Vitas Gerulaitis in straight sets for his third straight French title and fifth overall, he once again made the quick jump over the English Channel.

And then it happened...Borg defeated McEnroe in an epic five-set final (see incredible moment #2) to win his fifth straight Wimbledon title, and incredibly won the French Open and Wimbledon in the same year for the third year in a row. Bjorn would go on to win his sixth French Open in 1981, but it would be his last Grand Slam victory as he retired – are you ready for this? – after failing in his tenth attempt to win the US Open!

The Lovebird Double

Jimmy Connors and Chris Evert

Tennis's 60th most incredible moment occurred at Wimbledon in 1974. James Scott Connors and Christine Marie Evert both had tennis careers that have been admired by tennis fans and sports enthusiasts from around the world. These two legends actually had a lot in common. Both were fierce baseliners, relying heavily on their two-handed backhands, both were known for tenacity on the court, both stayed at the top of the tennis rankings for nearly two decades, and finally, both players ended up in the Tennis Hall of Fame. And the two all-time greats share one more common distinction; they were engaged to be married. In 1974 not only were the 21-year-old Connors and the 19-year-old Evert both flying high as arguably the best two players in the men's and women's games, but they were also in love. And as summer bloomed in June of 1974, both Jimmy and Chrissie came to England in search of their first Wimbledon crowns.

As the sport of tennis was enjoying one of its most popular years in 1974, a popular bet in the legalised betting venues of England was the 'Lovebird Double'. At 33-1 odds, many hopefuls put down their hard-earned cash in hopes of watching the two sweethearts win their respective singles titles. Those who took the wager on the unlikely double were initially shaken as Evert struggled in her first-round match. But showing the resolve that would eventually help her win 18 Grand Slam singles titles, Evert pulled out an 8-6, 5-7, 11-9 marathon over Leslie Hunt. This uncertain start would only prove to steel Evert's resolve as she made her way to the finals. There she soundly defeated the eighth-seeded Olga Morozova in straight sets, 6-0, 6-4, to win her first of three Wimbledon singles titles.

With Evert's work completed it was up to fiancé Jimmy to hold up his end of the bargain. Connors' big test came in the second round when he faced Australian Phil Dent. Although Connors had defeated Dent in the finals of the Australian Open earlier in the year in four sets, this match would prove to be different. Jimbo was a whisker from defeat in the fifth set when he served at 5-6, love-30 but, with typical gritty style, came back to win that service game and then pull out the victory. Connors then cruised until the quarters when he again needed five sets to triumph, this time over redoubtable Czech Jan Kodes. After defeating Dick Stockton in the semi-finals, Connors was one match away from the title and completing the second half of the Lovebird Double. Jimmy's last hurdle was sentimental favourite, 39-year-old Ken Rosewall. But this day proved to be all Connors.

And then it happened…the brash young Connors overwhelmed the old man 6-1, 6-1, 6-4. The Lovebirds had done it! They pulled off the only 'Lovebird Double' ever to grace the hallowed grounds of Wimbledon. And although Jimmy and Chrissie would call off their engagement before wedding bells rang, on this day in tennis, love actually stood for something after all.

Default or Disgrace?

Suzanne Lenglen v. Molla Mallory

Tennis's 59th most incredible moment occurred at the US Championships in 1921. This incident involved two extraordinary women, Suzanne Lenglen and Molla Mallory, who remain legendary in the history of the game. Lenglen, a Frenchwoman who is remembered as much for her flamboyant style as for her incredible play, was a player ahead of her time and truly one of the all-time greats. Her counterpart was Molla Mallory, a Norwegian-born player who emigrated to the United States in 1915. A great player in her own right, Mallory won the US Championships eight times. Despite the fact that her prime preceded Lenglen's by several years, their careers did briefly intersect. And luckily for the tennis world, the two great players met in the second round of the US Championships at Forest Hills.

Although Mallory was the defending champion, Lenglen had not lost a match as an amateur since World War I ended in 1918, and was clearly the favourite. Yet as the match got underway, Lenglen was bothered by constant coughing throughout the first set and appeared to be playing nervous tennis. To make matters worse for Madamoiselle Suzanne, Mallory was playing her usual consistent, intense game as she ran down and returned shot after shot. The result was a first set 6-2 victory for Mallory. As the second set started, Lenglen lost the first point to go down love-15 and then double faulted to fall behind love-30.

And then it happened...Lenglen began to cry, walked up to the chair umpire and stated that she was too ill to continue. She subsequently defaulted to lose her only match between 1919 and 1926. The crowd of 8,000, the largest US crowd ever to watch a women's tennis match, began to boo and hiss. The criticism became worse when Lenglen was seen the next day in perfect health attending several parties. Sentiment spread throughout tennis circles that Lenglen could not handle defeat and had defaulted rather than face being beaten in the traditional fashion. This loss turned out to be the only Grand Slam loss in Lenglen's illustrious amateur career. She ended with a record of 42 tournament victories and the single defeat to Mallory before turning professional at the end of 1926. And by the way, Mallory went on in the 1921 US Championship to defeat Mary Brown 4-6, 6-4, 6-2 for her sixth US title.

Did You See That?

Ellsworth Vines v. Bunny Austin

Tennis's 58th most incredible moment occurred at the 1932 Wimbledon final. Henry Ellsworth Vines Jr. was born on 29 September 1911 in Los Angeles, California. Vines, a slightly built 6′ 2″, 143-pound (64-kilo) beanpole was ironically best known for his powerful, go for broke game. Vines was fearless on the court. His flat, swift shots would not only graze the top of the net but would often land only inches inside the lines. Consequently, when Vines was in top form he could be as dominating as anyone who ever played. Conversely, when his dangerous shots were even slightly off their mark his game could crumble into ruins. And although Vines was known to have a powerful forehand, explosive overhead and solid volleys, his best shot was his legendary serve. A shot hit with extreme power and very little spin, it was similar to the rest of his game. When everything was clicking it could be as good as any player's, before or since. On the other hand, if all was not in sync the results could be quite ugly.

Fortunately for Vines, during the 1932 Wimbledon Championships his big game was falling beautifully into place. Vines cruised through the tournament and played terrific tennis, but as you will soon see he was obviously saving the best for last. Vines' final round opponent was the Englishman and hometown favourite Bunny Austin. As the final got underway, Vines was firing on all cylinders, clearly performing to his potential. Yet despite his flawless play, it all paled in comparison to the perfection of his serve. As Vines blasted ace after ace the overwhelmed Austin could do nothing but marvel at the greatness that was unfolding before his eyes. With Vines dominating 6-4, 6-2, 5-0 and serving for the match, the outcome was inevitable.

And then it happened...on match point Vines hit a serve with such pace and fury that, incredibly, Austin said after the match he couldn't tell whether the final serve went by him on his left or right side. The legendary Don Budge summed it up best when he stated, 'Thirty aces in 12 serving games. Considering it was against one of the finest players of the era, and a Wimbledon final, it could be the greatest serving demonstration ever.' Don, I couldn't agree more.

Dreams Can Come True

Andre Agassi v. Goran Ivanisevic

Tennis's 57th most incredible moment occurred at the 1992 Wimbledon Championships. Andre Kirk Agassi was born on 29 April 1970 in Las Vegas, Nevada. Andre's father, Emmanuel 'Mike' Agassi, was a former Olympic boxer of Armenian descent from Iran. And although Mike Agassi never made it to the big time, he had huge plans for his son. Legend has it that Mike put a tennis ball suspended from a string above Andre's crib and even tied a balloon to a ping pong paddle to help Andre with his hand-eye coordination when he was still too small to hold a full-sized racquet. As Andre's skill blossomed, he relocated to the Nick Bollettieri Tennis Academy at the age of 13. Three short years later he was ready for the professional ranks, and his talent and star power quickly launched him up the tennis ladder. As his game progressed, so did his endorsements. With his long bleach blond hair and flamboyant style, Andre appeared perfect for Hollywood and Madison Avenue. Yet as the years passed by he was unable to secure an elusive Grand Slam title. It was beginning to appear as if Andre was taking his Canon camera advert slogan of 'Image is everything' to heart. When he was upset in the final of the 1990 French Open by Andres Gomez, the 1990 US Open by Pete Sampras, and the 1991 French Open by Jim Courier, many sports enthusiasts began to ask the question, 'Can Agassi win the big one?'

As the 1992 Wimbledon championships approached, most 'tennis experts' didn't give Agassi a snowball's chance in hell. Even though he had reached the quarter-finals at the All England Club in 1991, Andre felt his game so ill-equipped for the grass courts of Wimbledon in the past that after losing in the first round in 1987 he had skipped the world's premier tournament for the next three years. Yet as he was making his way through the draw his confidence seemed to be growing with each victory. And when Andre defeated three-time Wimbledon champions, Boris Becker and John McEnroe in the quarter-finals and semi-finals respectively, he was poised to do the unthinkable, win at Wimbledon. But there was a formidable obstacle. Andre's opponent in the final would be the huge-serving Croat Goran Ivanisevic.

As the match got underway the tension was palpable. The Centre Court fans immediately sensed how desperately both players craved the title. No breaks of serve occurred in the first set, but Ivanisevic eventually took the early lead with a 10-8 tiebreak victory. Agassi, undeterred, even though Goran continued to fire off ace after ace (he would hit 37 aces in the finals and a record 206 for the tournament) fought back to take the next two sets 6-4, 6-4. But when Ivanisevic took the fourth set 6-1, it looked like Agassi's Grand Slam finals history might be repeating itself. Ivanisevic held a stellar 8-2 record in five set matches and had never lost a fifth set at Wimbledon. But Andre would hang tough in the deciding stanza and managed to grab the lead, 5-4.

At this point, while attempting to hold serve and even the match, Goran's nerves began to fail him. Double fault, love-15. Double fault, love -30. And although Ivanisevic was able to win the next point with a service winner, the door had been left open. At 15-30 Andre ripped a service return which set up a passing shot winner and he had two championship points. With the tension almost unbearable, Goran fought off the first championship point. With a second match point staring him in the face Ivanisevic put in his serve and came to net. Andre hit his return right up the middle.

And then it happened...Goran dumped his backhand volley in the net and it was over! Agassi fell face first onto the grass of Wimbledon's fabled Centre Court in a joyous celebration. As Andre went to embrace Goran at the net after their epic battle, Andre was seen mouthing the words 'I

Career Slam!

Andre Agassi v. Andrei Medvedev

Tennis's 56th most incredible moment occurred at the 1999 French Open. Andre Agassi was a true tennis prodigy, growing up on the hard courts of Las Vegas and then on both clay and hard surfaces at the Bollitieri Academy in Florida. Although Agassi made a big splash when he turned professional as a 16-year-old phenomenon, he had difficulty winning when it mattered most, at the Grand Slams. But after his historic breakthrough at Wimbledon in 1992 (see incredible moment #57) he was poised to make more Grand Slam history. Although his career had its ups and downs, by the time Andre reached the 1999 French Open he had already captured the US and Australian Open titles to go alongside his Wimbledon crown. Now, if Andre could pull out a title at the French, he would truly be making history by becoming only the fifth man ever to win all four Grand Slam events. And as if that were not enough, Agassi was vying to become the first man to win all four Grand Slams on three different surfaces. You see, when Perry, Budge, Emerson and Laver won their Grand Slam events, three of the four Grand Slams were on grass with only the French being on clay. But after Agassi won Wimbledon on grass and the US and Australian Opens on hard courts, if he could win the French on clay he would truly pull off a historic tennis first.

As the 13th-seeded Agassi cruised through the tournament and into the finals, the opponent waiting for him was also looking to make history. The Russian Andrei Medvedev had been ranked as high as four in the world in 1994, but after numerous injuries his ranking had dropped to a dismal #100 at the beginning of the 1999 French. Yet incredibly, Medvedev, resurrecting himself phoenix-like from the ashes, had battled his way all the way to his first Grand Slam finals. Furthermore, with his current ranking of 100, he was the lowest ranked player ever to reach the finals at Roland Garros. And although Andre was the heavy favourite to win the title, both players must have been acutely aware that in 1990 and 1991 Agassi was also the heavy favourite in the French title matches when he lost to Andres Gomez and Jim Courier, respectively.

As the Agassi-Medvedev final got underway, it appeared as if history would repeat itself as Medvedev took the first set 6-1 in a swift 19 minutes. The onslaught continued as he took the second set 6-2 for a commanding two-sets-to-love lead. But Andre knew that opportunities such as these don't come along every day. Gathering himself, Agassi kept battling and won the third set 6-4 and then the fourth 6-3 to even the finals at two sets apiece. With the A-Train rolling with a locomotive's momentum, he broke serve at two games all in the fifth and eventually held three championship points at five games to three. But Medvedev knew that he too was facing a once in a lifetime opportunity and staved off all three match points, winning the game to force Andre to serve out the victory.

After switching sides, the undeterred Agassi came out like a champion. Serving with power and precision, he took the advantage and soon the title was one stroke away. The next service exploded into Medvedev's forehand.

And then it happened...the pace was too much for Medvedev to handle, and his return sailed over the baseline. Andre burst into tears of joy. Agassi had done it! Ten years after his first Roland Garros finals appearance, Andre Agassi was a French Open champion and, in doing so, made tennis history.

Not Bad for an Old Man

Pancho Gonzalez v. Charlie Pasarell

Tennis's 55th most incredible moment occurred at Wimbledon in 1969. Ricardo Alonso 'Pancho' Gonzalez was born on 9 May 1928 in Los Angeles, California. As the story goes, little Pancho wanted a bicycle for his 12th birthday, but because his mother thought the gift too dangerous she gave him a tennis racquet instead. Pancho took to it immediately and so loved the game of tennis that he often skipped school to play. Ironically, due to his truancy he was forbidden from playing in junior tournaments in Southern California. Despite the ban, Pancho continued to play anywhere and everywhere until he spent a stint in the Navy during the years of 1945 and 1946. After leaving the military, Pancho was now of age and therefore allowed to play in amateur tournaments. He won the US championships at Forest Hills in 1948 and 1949, and subsequently tuned professional. After nearly 20 years in the pro ranks, where he won eight US Professional singles titles, the era of 'Open Tennis' was ushered in. In 1968 Gonzalez and the other 'professionals' were now allowed to once again enter the Grand Slam tournaments.

Although Gonzalez was now 40 years of age and well past his prime, he was still a formidable opponent. After a solid year in 1968, the 41-year-old Pancho faced Charlie Pasarell in the first round of the 1969 Wimbledon Championships. The match-up was unique for two reasons. Not only was Pasarell 16 years younger than Gonzalez, but Pancho had actually coached Pasarell as a junior player. As the match got underway on the first Tuesday of the tournament, one could sense that it was going to be a dog-fight. As the first set went on and on, Gonzalez, in a foreshadowing of things to come, staved off an incredible 11 set points before finally succumbing on the 12th when a lob sailed over his head, giving the first set to Pasarell 24 games to 22. At the conclusion of the lengthy and exhausting initial set, daylight began to dwindle and Gonzalez asked for play to be suspended until the next day. After several of his angry requests were denied, the irate 6' 3", 180-pound (80-kilo) Gonzalez was so frustrated that he barely went through the motions. As the crowd booed, Parasell took the second set in less than 15 minutes. Play was then suspended until the next day, but it appeared as if the damage had been done.

When the combatants came back the following day, however, a refreshed Gonzalez decided he was not yet ready to lie down and play dead. It was another gruelling set, but this time, when a nervous Pasarell threw in two double faults while serving at 14-15, Gonzalez was able to take the third set 16-14. Although Gonzalez may have seemed ageless to his opponent, he was obviously tiring but somehow managed to win the fourth set 6-3.

When it came down to the fifth set, it all appeared to be over when Pasarell held three match points with Gonzalez serving at 4-5, love 40.

And then it happened...Pancho fought off the match points to tie the set at 5 games all. But just as Gonzalez was able to take a deep breath of relief, Pasarell went ahead 6-5 and Pancho found himself once again facing three more match points while serving at love 40. Yet once again Pancho fought off the match points to even the score, this time at 6 games all. Incredibly, Pasarell held a seventh match point at 8-7, but Pancho would not be denied. In Houdini-like fashion he magically saved the seventh match point, and eventually went on to win all of the remaining points to take the longest match in Wimbledon history 22-24, 1-6, 16-14, 6-3, 11-9. The match lasted 112 total games, 19 more than the previous record played between Jaroslav Drobny and Budge Patty in 1953, and it endured an incredible five hours and 12 minutes. And Gonzalez wasn't finished yet. After the marathon with Pasarell, Gonzalez would go on to win his next two matches before losing to Arthur Ashe in the fourth round. Not bad for an old man...don't you think?

Ask Not What Your Country Can Do For You

John McEnroe v. Mats Wilander

Tennis's 54th most incredible moment occurred in the Davis Cup in 1982. As even the most casual of sports fans are aware, John Patrick McEnroe Jr. was one of the greatest tennis players ever to pick up a racquet. In his Hall of Fame career, McEnroe won three Wimbledon Championships and four US Open titles. And as if that were not enough, he is also considered to be the best doubles player of all time. But what many fans do not know is that John McEnroe was also one of the most patriotic tennis players ever to play for his country.

The Davis Cup, founded in 1900 by Dwight Davis, is a team competition that pits country against country. Unfortunately, in today's ‘me’ society, many top players don't always play Davis Cup events because they feel that it might have a negative impact on their individual careers. Yet from day one, McEnroe always made playing for his country a priority. And as they say, the statistics don't lie. Johnny Mac holds the US Davis Cup records for the most singles matches played with 49, the most singles victories with 41, and total victories with 59. And in addition, the most total matches played with 69, the most ties played with 30, and the most years on the team with 12...now that's what I call dedication. Yet when the defending champion US team, led by none other than John McEnroe, faced Sweden in a quarter-final match-up in 1982, no one could have predicted what was in store for the native from Douglaston, NY.

Although McEnroe had done his part with a singles victory over Anders

Jarryd and a doubles victory for a second point, his teammates lost the other two matches to the Swedes. That left John to play Mats Wilander in the deciding match. In today's Davis Cup competition, like all of the Grand Slam tournaments except the US Open, there are no tiebreakers in the final set of play. But back in 1982, when men were men, there were no tiebreakers in any of the sets. You had to win the old fashion way, by a margin of two games.

Neither man would give an inch, and as the first set was extended to extra games it was a foreshadowing of things to come. McEnroe eventually won the first, 9-7, and took control of the match by winning the second set six games to two. Although things looked desperate for Sweden, they were playing in their home country and did have their best player on the court. Wilander, evidently spurred on by the partisan home crowd support, fought back to win an agonisingly long third set 17-15. Now with the momentum behind him, Mats went on to win the fourth set 6-3 to the joy of the Swedish fans.

Now the Davis Cup tie came down to one final set. The two players were already exhausted by the long match, but with the championship at stake, both men were committed to leaving everything on the court. After what seemed to be an eternity, McEnroe, leading seven games to six, finally reached match point.

And then it happened...after six hours and 32 minutes of play, John McEnroe won the final point of what is still to this day the longest singles Davis Cup match ever played, and subsequently fell into the arms of his captain Arthur Ashe and his trainer Bill Norris. Game, Set and Match USA! And as an apparent encore, after leading the US past Australia in the Davis Cup semi-finals, McEnroe was the impetus as the United States defended its Davis Cup title when he defeated Yannick Noah in a – get this – five set, four-hour-and-21 minute match as the US defeated France 4-1.

Over his tumultuous career, John McEnroe has had his detractors, and much of their criticism was deserved by his boorish behaviour on court. But one thing cannot be denied. When it came to patriotic commitment, Johnny Mac was there, and in spades. Now that's what I call *serving* your country.

From Triumph to Tragedy

Bill Tilden

Tennis's 53rd most incredible moment occurred in 1949. It all started on 10 February 1893 when William T. Tilden II was born into a wealthy Philadelphia family. Eventually, 'Big Bill' was destined to become one of the greatest tennis champions in the history of the sport. Yet few would have predicted Tilden's future greatness when his career got off to a rocky start. In Big Bill's first significant tournament, he lost at Newport in 1912 in the first round to Wallace Johnson. Truth be told, Tilden wouldn't win his first Grand Slam event until he won Wimbledon in 1920 at the ancient tennis age of 27. But it was at this point that the 6′ 2″, 155-pound (70-kilo) future icon's career was about to take off. As Tilden was working hard to hone his skills, his tennis game was going into overdrive. In the 1920s, Tilden would not lose a significant tennis match for an astonishing seven years!

Eventually, he would amass seven straight US singles championships (a record which still stands today) and three Wimbledon crowns. He also won two professional titles and 21 of 28 Davis Cup matches in his illustrious career. Tilden became so dominant that at times he would play to his opponents' strengths and mimic their style of play, just to make things more competitive.

To go along with Tilden's great physical gifts, he was a highly intelligent player as well. Tilden wrote three books on the game, *How to*

Play Better Tennis, *The Art of Lawn Tennis* and *Match Play and the Spin of the Ball*, all of which were very well received. But despite his athletic greatness and superstar status, Tilden had one cross to bear. In the highly homophobic society of the second quarter of the twentieth century, Tilden was discovered to be homosexual. As his lifestyle became more and more apparent, he was eventually barred from playing in a number of tournaments.

And then it happened...in 1947 Tilden was sentenced to one year in prison for 'contributing to the delinquency of a minor'. And although he would serve only six months of this one-year sentence, he would eventually be convicted again in 1949 for a parole violation when he made unwanted advances and fondled a hitchhiking teenage boy. (This time he spent approximately 10 months in jail.) But as a testament to Tilden's greatness, just six weeks after getting out of prison for the second time, in a landslide vote the Associated Press named Tilden the greatest tennis player of the first half of the twentieth century.

Unfortunately, things did not turn out well for Big Bill. After squandering his fortune, Tilden had to sell many of his trophies just to survive. In 1953 he died of a heart attack in a Los Angeles hotel room. At the time, he had been on his way to the US Championships. Sadly, arguably the greatest tennis champion the sport has ever known was said to have less than $100 dollars in the bank at the time of his death.

If You Can Make It There, You Can Make It Anywhere

Jimmy Connors

Tennis's 52nd most incredible moment occurred at the 1978 US Open. James Scott Connors Jr. was born on 2 September 1952 in St Louis, Illinois. Raised by his tennis teaching professional mother, Jimmy was playing the game that would make him famous by the time he was two. Connors was not the most talented youth on the block, and furthermore he was always small for his age. Consequently, he had to fight twice as hard as his opponents to win a match. The results of these hard efforts produced one of the grittiest, most fiery, and mentally toughest players ever to grace the sport. Jimmy would never give up, would never say die. And largely due to his steely will, Connors went on to have one of the most heralded tennis careers of all time.

Although Jimmy was always at 110 percent, his rough, tough, in-your-face attitude seemed to work best in front of the electric US Open crowds. Jimmy first reached the US Open finals in 1974 when, as an upstart 22-year-old, he blew away the sentimental favourite Ken Rosewall in the grass court final 6-1, 6-0, 6-1 for his third major of the year. (See incredible moment #82.) After losing the 1975 US Open finals to Manuel Orantes in straight sets (see incredible moment #70) he made his way back to the finals for a third straight year in 1976 and defeated his rival Bjorn Borg, this time on clay, in a match which saw Jimbo take an epic third-set tiebreaker and the title 6-4, 3-6, 7-6 (11-9), 6-4. Jimmy would reach the US Open final for a fourth consecutive year in 1977 but would lose to Guillermo Vilas in four sets, this time dropping the swing third set tiebreaker. And incredibly, the fighting battler from Illinois would reach his fifth straight US Open final in 1978, the most since Bill Tilden reached eight consecutive US finals from 1918-1925, but not before he was down 5-4, 30-all to the Italian Adriano Panatta in the fifth set of the fourth round on Panatta's serve. Yet as would be Jimmy's MO he came out of the corner punching. After breaking Panatta's serve and holding his own, Jimmy would hit one of the most memorable shots in tennis history, a one-handed running backhand winner around the net post with the score at 5-6 and deuce. Subsequently, the disheartened Panatta double faulted to give Jimbo the final set 7-5. Connors would later say that this win over Panatta gave him the momentum he needed for the rest of the tournament.

After taking out Brian Gottfried in the quarter-finals and John McEnroe in the semis, both in straight sets, Connors was vying to make history. If Jimmy could defeat Bjorn Borg in the inaugural finals at the National Tennis Center in Flushing Meadows on the newly paved hard courts, Connors would be the first man, and conceivably the only man, ever to win the US Open on three different surfaces. But this would be no easy feat for the American. Just several months earlier Borg had dominated Connors in the Wimbledon finals in straight sets, and to make things more foreboding the amazing Swede was riding a 39-match winning streak. But the US Open would prove to be Borg's Achilles heel and he quickly went down to Connors two sets to love. Now Jimmy sensed blood, and as always he went in for the kill. Connors was cruising in the third with a 5-2 advantage.

And then it happened...Jimmy took the final game and the title for a third time, 6-4, 6-2, 6-2, and had made history by winning the US Open on three different surfaces. Jimmy would go on to win the US Open two more times, in 1982 and 1983, for a total of five US Open titles. And although he also won two Wimbledon championships and one Australian crown, Jimmy Connors always felt most at home in his home country...at the US Open!

The MIdas Touch

Steffi Graf

Tennis's 51st most incredible moment occurred in 1988. Steffi Graf had a career that few have ever paralleled. She won a total of 22 Grand Slam titles and is the only man or woman ever to win each Grand Slam at least four times. And as if that were not enough, she also holds the women's record with 186 consecutive weeks as the world's number one. But by far, the crowning jewel on Steffi's tiara was a 1988 season that will always be the benchmark for future greats to come. It all started for the 18-year-old teenager at the year's first Grand Slam, the Australian Open, where she cruised to the title without the loss of a single set. It was then on to the French Open. After a tense semi-final match-up with Gabriela Sabatini she demolished the surprise finalist Natalia Zvereva, 6-0, 6-0 in an embarrassing 32-minute final. (See incredible moment #89.) The next stop was Wimbledon, which most experts felt would be Graf's biggest obstacle due to the grass court greatness of none other than Martina Navratilova. And surprise, surprise it was Navratilova who would end up being Graf's opponent in the finals.

As the match got underway it looked to all as if Martina would indeed upend Graf's Grand Slam hopes when she raced out to a 7-5, 2-0 lead. Yet just as things were starting to look desperate for Steffi, she stepped it up a couple of notches, conceded only one more game throughout the rest of the match, and ran away with the title, 5-7, 6-2,

6-1. Now all that stood between Graf and becoming the fifth player in the history of the game to win all four majors in the same calendar year was the US Open. As Graf reached the finals, her record for the year to date was an astonishing 61 wins and only 2 defeats. And as fate would have it, the woman who had given Graf the two blemishes on her record was none other than her finals opponent, Gabriela Sabatini. But even an uncharacteristically nervous Graf was not to be denied as she secured the Grand Slam title by defeating Sabatini 6-3, 3-6, 6-1 (50 years after Don Budge first won the first Grand Slam – see incredible moment #13).

Amazingly, Graf's incredible year was not yet complete. As fate would have it, the Olympics had included tennis as a medal sport for the first time since 1924. So it was off to Seoul.

And then it happened...in a repeat of the US Open final, Graf once again defeated Sabatini, thereby becoming the first man or woman to win the Grand Slam and an Olympic gold medal in the same year, a feat that eventually came to be known as the 'Golden Slam'. In a career characterised by one history making moment after another, this was her pinnacle, her tour de force, her golden moment...her Golden Slam.

Our Ginny

Virginia Wade v. Betty Stove

Tennis's 50th most incredible moment occurred in the 1977 Wimbledon Ladies Final. Sarah Virginia Wade was born on 10 July 1945 in Bournemouth. Like all English tennis players, Wade had one main goal, to someday win her country's national championship, Wimbledon. Even though she had been a perennial top ten player since 1967, and reached a career high of number two in the world in 1968, she had yet to achieve her dream of obtaining a Wimbledon singles title despite 15 previous attempts. Yet if there was ever such a thing as a fairy tale in tennis, this would be Wade's year. For not only was it the centenary anniversary of the championships, but the Queen was also celebrating her Silver Jubilee year and consequently was gracing the tournament with a rare appearance. Buoyed on by the partisan crowd, 'Our Ginny', as she was affectionately referred to, reached the semi-finals of Wimbledon for the third time. Ominously for Wade, her opponent this day was the world's number one and defending champion, Chris Evert. But the inspired Wade was up to the task. She dismissed Evert by the score of 6-2, 4-6, 6-1 in an effort Wade described as 'my best match of the tournament and possibly my career'.

Because English tennis champions were a rarity, and because no Brit had won Wimbledon since Ann Jones did so eight years earlier in 1969, the crowd was desperate to see 'Our Ginny' take the title. Wade's opponent in the final was the 6 foot, 160-pound (72-kilo) Betty Stove of the Netherlands. With the pressure squarely on the shoulders of the 5' 8" Wade, Stove took the first set 6-4. But it appeared on this day that a storybook ending could not be denied.

And then it happened...Wade fought back to take the final two sets and the championship by the score of 4-6, 6-3, 6-1. The overjoyed crowd of over 14,000 was in a state of ecstasy as they sang in unison, 'For She's a Jolly Good Fellow!' In a tournament that was the defining moment in her career, Wade was asked after the match if she had come down from cloud nine. Wade's response was simple and to the point. 'No I haven't,' she replied. 'I never will.'

Just Say No!

Nikki Pilic

Tennis's 49th most incredible moment occurred during the Wimbledon Championships in 1973. This episode in tennis history began when the Yugoslavian Tennis Association suspended their country's #1 player, Nikki Pilic, for three months. The alleged infraction was allegedly backing out of a commitment to play in the Davis Cup, even though Pilic vehemently denied ever making such a commitment. The newly formed Association of Tennis Professionals (ATP) objected to the suspension and threatened to boycott the upcoming French Open if the suspension was not lifted. The ATP then appealed the case to the International Lawn Tennis Federation (currently called the International Tennis Federation, or ITF) which shortened the suspension to one month. Yet when the appeal process was finally finished, although the suspension was now substantially shorter, it would still keep Pilic out of the longest standing, most traditional of all tournaments...Wimbledon.

Needless to say, this scenario did not sit well with the ATP. The members of the new union felt that if they did not stand up to the ITF now, they would be setting an ominous precedent for the future. As time passed and push came to shove, neither side would blink.

And then it happened...as the Wimbledon fortnight was about to begin and the ITF would not lift Pilic's suspension, the ATP members did the unthinkable; they voted to boycott the All England Championships.

Seventy-nine of the best tennis players in the world, including 13 of the 16 seeds, withdrew from Wimbledon, leaving a decimated tournament draw. Yet due to the fact that several of the top players, including Nastase, Connors, Borg, Kodes, and the favourite English son, Roger Taylor, decided to play, as well as the fact that this was, after all, Wimbledon, the crowds still came out in record numbers. But when top-seeded Nastase lost in the fourth round, Borg lost in the quarter-finals, and Taylor and Connors were defeated in the semis, it lead to an anti-climatic final in which Jan Kodes of Czechoslovakia defeated Alex Metreveli of Russia in straight sets. And although Kodes won two French Open titles and achieved a career-high ranking of number five in the world, he will always be remembered first and foremost as 'The Wimbledon Boycott Champion'.

Sweet SIxteen

Tracy Austin v. Chris Evert

Tennis's 48th most incredible moment occurred at the 1979 US Open. Tracy Ann Austin was born on 12 December 1962 in Palos Verdes, California and was one of the first tennis prodigies of the Open Era. After winning an incredible 25 junior tournaments, young Tracy had accomplished all she could in the amateur ranks. Consequently, at the tender age of 14, the 5 foot, 90-pound (40-kilo) girl in pigtails turned pro and unbelievably won the first professional tournament she entered. With the tennis world as her oyster, Austin continued to climb the charts. She became the youngest player ever to gain entry into Wimbledon and the US Open, and the youngest player ever to be ranked within the top ten US women. Then, in 1978, Austin climbed another step up the tennis ladder by breaking into the top ten players in the world. The following year, in 1979, the 16-year-old California girl was ready to take the ultimate step, to become a Grand Slam champion.

After reaching the semi-finals at Wimbledon, Tracy made her way to Flushing Meadows for the US Open. The self-assured teenager was cruising through the draw and reached the finals brimming with confidence. Although many older, more experienced players have wilted in the presence of their first Grand Slam final, Tracy was poised for the opportunity of a lifetime. Facing the perennial US Open powerhouse and four time defending champion Chris Evert, Austin came out firing. After winning a tight first set, six games to four, Austin never let up. Playing like a Chrissie clone with a patented two-fisted backhand of her own, Tracy went ahead five games to three in the second set.

And then it happened... Tracy Austin took the final game and the title 6-4, 6-3. At the age of 16 years and nine months, Austin surpassed Maureen Connolly's 1951 effort to become the youngest US Open champion in the history of the tournament. And in a foreshadowing of things to come, a 20-year-old youngster named John Patrick McEnroe Jr. became the youngest US champion on the men's side since Pancho Gonzalez claimed the title back in 1948.

Although a variety of injuries cut Austin's career short, she was still able to secure a second US Open title in 1981 and eventually, in 1992, at the age of 29 years and seven months, extended her string of firsts by becoming the youngest inductee into the Tennis Hall of Fame.

Court Holds Court

Margaret Court

Tennis's 47th most incredible moment occurred in 1975, but in reality, like all of these stories, this was truly a lifetime in the making. Margaret Smith Court was born on 16 July 1942 in the town of Albury in New South Wales. Unlike today's tennis superstars who are all too often swinging a tennis racquet before they can sing their ABC's, young Margaret didn't pick up the game until the ancient age of eight. But Margaret Smith (she didn't become Margaret Smith Court until she married Barry Court in 1967) was a tenacious worker and her game seemed to grow as quickly as her 5′ 11″ of height. By 1960, only ten years after she struck her first ball, the 18-year-old New Zealander won her first Grand Slam title by taking the Australian Open.

If what they say is true, and winning is in fact contagious, then Margaret Smith Court should be quarantined before she infects all of New Zealand. Although truth be told I guess it's a good bet that almost every player who has ever had aspirations of holding up a Grand Slam trophy wouldn't have minded if Court gave a cough in their direction. You see, after winning that first Grand Slam, the elegant serve and volleyer went on to win six more Australian singles titles in a row, and 11 overall. But Court didn't save all of her winning just for the home folk. On the contrary, she spread the wealth. As Court was winning in Australia she was simultaneously racking up singles, doubles and mixed doubles Grand

Slam victories at all four of the Grand Slam events. And even after a short layoff following her marriage in 1967, Court came back to have the best years of her career.

After winning three of the four Grand Slams in 1969 (she lost in the semis of Wimbledon to eventual champion Ann Jones) she came back in 1970 at the age of 28 to win the Australian, French, Wimbledon – in a thrilling final over Billie Jean King (see incredible moment #14) – and eventually won her second calendar Grand Slam by defeating Rosie Casals in three sets in the US Open finals. (That's right, you heard me, it was Court's second calendar Grand Slam. In 1963 she teamed up with Australian Ken Fletcher to win the mixed doubles Grand Slam.) And when 1970 had finally come to a close, Court had compiled a record of 104 wins to only 6 defeats while winning 21 of 27 tournaments. Compared to Connolly's Grand Slam year of 1953, when she played only 12 tournaments, and Graf's Grand Slam year of 1988, when she only played 14 tournaments, Court's feat was truly monumental. And unbelievably, Court just kept on winning. Even after the birth of her first of three children in 1973, Court kept the gravy train trucking along.

And then it happened...Margaret Smith Court teamed up with Virginia Wade of England to defeat Billie Jean King and Rosie Casals for the US Open doubles title in 1975. In doing so, Court won her record 62nd and final Grand Slam victory. When all was said and done, in Margaret Smith Court's 18-year career she finished the year with the world's top ranking seven times and was inducted into the tennis Hall of Fame in 1979. (Now that's a lot of time spent on the court!) And considering how today's modern players concentrate their efforts primarily on singles play, Court's record will most likely be around for years to come.

Bombs Away

Bill Tilden

Tennis's 46th most incredible moment occurred in 1931. William Tatem Tilden II is considered one of the greatest players ever to play the game. Born on 10 February 1893, Big Bill was the winner of 21 Grand Slam titles, ten in singles, before turning professional in 1931. From the years of 1920 through 1926 Tilden dominated the sport with great athleticism and a keen tennis mind. Although Bill was known to play a cerebral game, approaching every match with a chess-like mentality and dissecting every point like a surgeon, he was best known for his huge serve. Tilden, who stood 6' 2" tall with a V-shaped torso, had the quintessential tennis body. Big Bill used his god-given ability to develop a 'cannonball' first serve and a deadly 'American twist' second serve that was second to none.

In retrospect, Tilden's powerful serve was a predecessor to the big servers of the twenty-first century. Players like Sampras, Roddick and the Williams sisters all followed in the footsteps of the legendary Tilden. Yet throughout the history of the game, there have been many recorded swift serves. For example, in the 1930s Lester Rollo Stoeten had a serve clocked at 131 mph. And then in 1963, the Englishman Mike Sangster unleashed a 154 mph bomb. More recently, Greg Rusedski recorded a 155 mph monster and Venus Williams launched a 127 mph rocket, a women's record. But tennis's 46th most incredible moment occurred in 1931. Tilden was playing in a match in his first year as a professional.

And then it happened... Big Bill stepped up to the line and served up an unbelievable, record-setting 163 mph missile. Of course there is some scepticism about the technology used for measuring serving speed at the time, but what makes this feat even more astonishing is that while today's players are using racquets made of such high tech materials as graphite and titanium, which add considerable power to one's strokes, Tilden hit his with a mere wooden frame. Fittingly, in 1959, Tilden served his way right into the International Tennis Hall of Fame.

I Can't Take the Pressure!

M.H. de Amorin v. L.B. Thung

Tennis's 45th most incredible moment occurred at Wimbledon in 1957. Anyone who has played sports on any level has undoubtedly felt the pressures of competition. Whether it is a Grand Slam final or simply your weekend tennis match, nerves and stress have, and always will, play a pivotal role. Due to the fact that tennis is an individual sport and the players are normally on the court with nobody to rely on but themselves, the pressure of the game can, at times, be overwhelming. There have been countless examples of nerves getting to professional tennis players. From serving underhand to anxiety attacks on the court, players will continue to succumb to the pressures of the game. Consequently, tennis players and fans alike have come up with many terms to try to express just what the players are going through. Examples include the ever-popular 'choke', 'gag' and 'collapse', which are popular favourites in tennis and all of sports. You also have the expressions that are specifically pertinent to tennis such as 'lead elbow', 'feet stuck in cement' and countless others. And, of course, the more important the moment, the greater is the likelihood of a serious meltdown.

In our sport there is no more important happening than a Grand Slam event. And this leads us to our 45th most incredible moment in tennis. The scene was the first round at Wimbledon in 1957. M.H. de Amorin was a player from Brazil who had trained her whole life to reach this moment, her first Wimbledon match. She was undoubtedly excited and nervous, and like all players, simply hoped to perform at her best on this most auspicious of occasions. Amorin's opponent on this day was L.B. Thung of Holland, but on this day Thung would be the least of Amorin's problems. The match got underway and Amorin nervously came out to serve.

And then it happened... Double fault, love-15. Double fault, love-30. Double fault, love-40. Double fault, game. Amorin came out in the next service game and it was a repeat performance. And the next service game was the same...and then another game of four double faults. All in all, the incredible choke ended after a mind-blowing 17 consecutive double faults! Not surprisingly, Amorin lost the match even though she was able to pull it together long enough to win one set and make the score a somewhat respectable 6-3, 4-6, 6-1. Sadly, the contest that Amorin had most likely dreamed about her entire life ended in one of the biggest nightmares any players has ever encountered on the court.

Always Try Your Best

Marat Safin v. Grant Stafford

Tennis's 44th most incredible moment occurred at the 2000 Australian Open. Marat Safin appeared destined from birth to become a tennis champion. His mother, Raisa, was a former top ten women's player in Russia and his father, Mikhail, managed a local tennis club. As the story goes, little Marat would accompany his parents to the club as soon as he could hold a racquet and by the age of five was playing alongside none other than Anna Kournikova. As Marat's abilities progressed, the 6' 4'', 195-pound (88-kilo) man-child was eventually ready for the big time and turned professional in 1997. Safin indubitably had the physical tools to become one of the game's elite players. The question was whether or not the temperamental Russian could keep it together psychologically day in and day out.

Throughout the early years of Safin's career his results were mixed, flashes of greatness followed by episodes of self-destruction. Despite his prodigious talent, in 1999 he reached only the third round of the Australian Open. In 2000 he arrived at this event apparently poised and ready to go. But the key word here is 'apparently'.

Safin's first-round match seemed routine enough. His opponent was the lightly regarded South African qualifier Grant Stafford. As the match got underway, all was going according to form. It was a tight first set but almost all in attendance simply assumed that Marat would 'turn it on' when need be. The key word this time being 'assumed', because Stafford had his own ideas and ended up winning the first set in a tiebreaker. As a discouraged Safin started the second set, his energy and will to play seemed to be sapped from his body. His unforced errors quickly mounted and his effort waned, causing the American umpire Norm Chryst to have no alternative but to warn Safin for his 'lack of effort'. And after Marat lost the second set 6-4 and was getting pummelled in the third, Chryst had to warn Safin repeatedly. By the time the match mercifully came to an end, 6-1 in the third set, Safin had committed 43 unforced errors to only seven winners and had been warned on four separate occasions to try harder.

And then it happened...in the well over 100 years of Grand Slam competition, Marat Safin earned the infamous distinction of becoming the first player to be fined for a 'lack of effort'. Yet this story has a happy ending, for it appeared that Safin had learned a valuable lesson. After his embarrassing display in the Australian Open, he turned his attitude around completely and later that year won his first Grand Slam event when he upset Pete Sampras in the finals of the 2000 US Open. And believe it or not, Safin even went on to win the Australian Open five years later in 2005, with a monumental effort where he defeated the great Roger Federer in the semis after facing a match point, and the hometown favourite Hewitt in the final.

The Energiser Bunny

Ken Rosewall

Tennis's 43rd most incredible moment occurred in 1971. Born on 2 November 1934, Kenneth Robert Rosewall had a career that spanned three decades. Ironically nicknamed 'Muscles' by his countrymen, Rosewall was a 5' 7'', 140-pound (63-kilo) Australian who loved to play the game. Rosewall began his tennis playing days as an amateur and found immediate success. As a teenager Muscles was already a Grand Slam champion, winning the French and Australian singles championships in 1953. He would follow up those victories with another Australian victory in 1955, and a US Championship in 1956, before turning professional in 1957. While playing professionally, Rosewall, like the other touring pros, was banned from the Grand Slam events until tennis eventually opened its doors to all comers in 1968. By the time the Open Era rolled around, Rosewall had been ineligible to play for tennis's most prestigious titles for 11 years in the prime of his career.

In 1968 Rosewall was 33 years old. Yet even at this advanced tennis age, 'Muscles' still had plenty left in his tank. He started right away by winning the '68 French Open. He then went on to win the US Championship for the second time in 1970. Yet it would be at the 1971 Australian Open that tennis's 43rd most incredible moment would take place. Rosewall, now ancient in tennis terms, was 36 years of age. Australian by birth, Rosewall was attempting to win his nation's Grand

Slam event 18 years after originally winning it in 1953. And he started off well, making it all the way to the quarter-finals without losing a single set. But as they say, with the best players still to come, 'this is where they separate the men from the boys'. Rosewell faced Roy Emerson in the quarters and continued his brilliant play, winning again in straight sets by the score of 6-4, 6-4, 6-3. He then faced Tom Okker in the semi-finals. Playing as well as ever he won again, this time without dropping a set by the scores of 6-2, 7-6, 6-4.

Now the old man of the tournament had one final hurdle, the great Arthur Ashe who was playing on grass, his favourite surface.

And then it happened...Ken 'Muscles' Rosewall swept through Ashe and the finals 6-1, 7-5, 6-3. Rosewall had done the inconceivable. He had won a Grand Slam tournament at the age of 36 without losing a single set! Not too shabby for an old man. Oh, did I forget to mention...as an encore, Rosewall defended his Australian Open title the following year at the age of 37!

When 'Class' Met the 'Ass'

Arthur Ashe v. Ille Nastase

Tennis's 42nd most incredible moment occurred during the year-ending Masters tournament in 1975. Arthur Ashe was arguably the greatest ambassador the game of tennis has ever seen. A man of dignity and class, Ashe was a true gentleman on and off the court. Despite an outstanding career which saw him become the only African-American male to win a Grand Slam singles event (the US Open in 1968, the Australian Open in 1970, and Wimbledon in 1975), he will be remembered as much for the manner in which he comported himself in the face of racism and adversity as for his triumphs on the court.

And then there was Ilie Nastase, aptly nicknamed 'Nasty' due to his terrible on-court behaviour. Nastase was as talented a player as has ever played the game. When he was focused and his emotions were under control, which was seldom, he produced some of the most spectacular tennis of his generation. Yet in a career that saw him win two Grand Slam singles titles (the US Open in 1972 and the French Open in 1973) and hold down the world's number one ranking in 1973, Ilie 'Nasty' Nastase will likely be remembered as much for his antics and outbursts as for his tennis brilliance.

This leads us to the 1975 Masters tournament in Stockholm. The Masters is a round robin event that is limited to the top eight players in the world at the end of each tennis season. The eight players compete in two groups of four. The two players in each group with the best records then advance to the semi-finals. Tennis's 42nd most incredible moment occurred during a round robin match-up between Ashe and Nastase. As the match began, Nastase appeared to be in rare form, behaving even nastier than his normal self. Throughout the match Nastase was arguing, berating the lines people, throwing his racquet, cursing, and basically acting like a complete brat in general. Enduring one tantrum after another, the dignified Ashe just continued to play, seemingly undeterred. Nastase took the first set 6-1 and Ashe fought back to win the second 7-5. Finally, in the third set, Ashe was leading by four games to one and was in command of the match.

And then it happened... Nastase began to argue and stall for the umpteenth time. Finally the unflappable Ashe had had enough. In a stunning turn of events Ashe put down his racquet and walked off the court. The referee for the match, Horst Klosterkemper, pleaded with Ashe to continue playing but Arthur wouldn't hear of it. Klosterkemper then disqualified Nastase. Now there was the implausible situation where both men would get a loss on their records. Thankfully the powers that be came to their senses the next day and awarded Ashe the victory. But then, because it was a double elimination tournament, Nastase was still able to advance to the semi-final round where he defeated Guillermo Vilas and, you guessed it, ended up taking the title by dismantling Bjorn Borg in the finals 6-2, 6-2, 6-1.

It is said that nice guys finish last. Over the course of his stellar career, the highly regarded Arthur Ashe belied this notion. But on this day it held true; the nice guy really did finish last.

Tears for Tim

Pete Sampras v. Jim Courier

Tennis's 41st most incredible moment occurred at the 1995 Australian Open. It all started when the world's number one player, Pete Sampras, was practising early in the tournament with his long-time coach and friend, Tim Gullikson. During this practice session Gullikson suddenly collapsed on the court and was immediately rushed to hospital. Unfortunately the medical tests revealed a brain tumour and Gullikson flew back to the US to start treatment just before Sampras's quarter-final match with fellow American Jim Courier. As the Sampras-Courier quarter-final match-up began, Pete's mind was obviously with his coach while his body was on the tennis court in Melbourne. When Sampras lost the first set in a tiebreaker, seven games to six, his chances didn't look good. Things quickly went from bad to worse when he lost the second in a tiebreaker as well. Now Pete was in the unenviable position of facing one of the world's best players, trailing two sets to love, and fighting the heartbreaking emotions of knowing his coach was struggling for his life. Yet somehow he was able to continue competing at a high level and came back to win the third set 6-3. Incredibly, he won the fourth set as well, evening the match at two sets all.

And then it happened... as the players were giving all they had in the fifth and final set a fan yelled out to Sampras, 'Do it for your coach'. Well that was more than the normally reserved Sampras could take. When he and Courier were sitting at the changeover between games, Sampras broke down into tears. As the players resumed their match, Pete began to play what can only be called a paradox of tennis brilliance. Sampras was weeping on the court and yet was unbelievably able to wipe away the tears just long enough to serve up an ace or unleash a winner. Courier, Sampras's friend and opponent, graciously offered to finish the match the next day. At first Sampras thought the gesture was disingenuous, but soon realised it was sincere. Pete then played on through the tears and the heartache to win the fifth set and the match 6-7, 6-7, 6-3, 6-4, 6-3. Sampras, who many media types had labelled as boring, put on one of the finest displays of guts and glory that has ever been seen in the history of the sport. Sadly, Gullikson would eventually succumb to the brain tumour. But on this one day in Australia, Pete Sampras paid as fine a tribute to his coach and friend as any that has ever been witnessed. The reserved Sampras put it simply after the match. 'That was one of the better matches I've ever taken part in. I'm proud I didn't quit.'

Never Talk About a Man's Mother

John McEnroe v. Mikael Pernfors

Tennis's 40th most incredible moment occurred at the 1990 Australian Open. John McEnroe was having one of his most successful Grand Slams in years. McEnroe hadn't won a major title since 1984 but now, in Melbourne, McEnroe was playing well and was involved in a fourth-round encounter with tenacious Swede Mikael Pernfors. And although John was leading by two games to one in the third set, he appeared to be in another one of his ornery moods. As the players switched ends, McEnroe began to stare at a lineswoman whom he believed had given him a bad call two games earlier. The umpire, Gerry Armstrong, observed this act of intimidation and promptly gave McEnroe a warning for unsportsmanlike conduct. Despite the warning, McEnroe secured the third set 7-5 to take a two sets to one lead. As play continued into the fourth set and McEnroe was serving at 2-3, he made an unforced error which put him a break point down. The perturbed McEnroe then slammed his racquet onto the court in anger. Although Mac had thrown his racquet several times previously in the match, this time it cracked. According to the rules, destroying a racquet as a result of an angry outburst is grounds for an automatic racquet abuse violation. Since this was McEnroe's second violation of the match, it warranted a point penalty which resulted in giving Pernfors a crucial break of serve for a 4-2 advantage. McEnroe argued that the racquet only had a small crack and therefore was still useable. Consequently he felt that he didn't deserve a penalty and asked to see the tournament referee Ken Ferrar. When Ferrar backed up Armstrong's ruling, McEnroe very eloquently told him to 'Just go f*** your mother!'

And then it happened...Gerry Armstrong uttered the phrase, 'Verbal obscenity, Mr McEnroe. Disqualification. Game, Set and Match, Mr. Pernfors.' John McEnroe had done it! He had become the first player to earn such a disqualification from a major championship since the Open Era began in 1968. After the match McEnroe admitted that he hadn't realised that the disqualification rules had been changed. Previously a player was disqualified on his fourth offence, but as of 1 January of that year a player was to be defaulted on his third. In effect, McEnroe's ignorance cost him the match and a chance at another Grand Slam title. Afterwards McEnroe said about the disqualification, 'It was bound to happen sometime. I don't feel good about it, but I can't say I'm totally surprised.' McEnroe, who for all intents and purposes retired shortly thereafter, never did win another Grand Slam title but I'm sure he learned a valuable lesson...Never, *ever* talk about another man's mother.

Fire and Ice

Bjorn Borg v. Vitas Gerulaitis

Tennis's 39th most incredible moment occurred in the 1977 Wimbledon semi-finals. 1977 was a very special year for the Championships because they were celebrating their 100th anniversary. And although the anniversary tournament is often remembered for the Englishwoman Virginia Wade's historic victory (see incredible moment #50), the semi-final match-up between Vitas Gerulaitis and Bjorn Borg is considered by many to be one of the greatest matches ever played on Centre Court.

Vitas Gerulaitis was the ultimate American playboy. With an affinity for money, cars (he had two Rolls Royces), partying and women, 'Broadway Vitas', as the media dubbed him, liked to live on the edge and his tennis game often followed suit. In contrast, Bjorn Borg appeared to be the antithesis of everything Vitas stood for. On and off the courts, Borg was a quiet man whose game also seemed to mirror his personality. In this case, however, opposites attracted, and the two men were not only often practice partners, but good friends as well. Yet on this day the off-court relationship was placed on hold as the two opponents were prepared to do whatever it took to gain a treasured spot in the finals.

As the match got underway the play was top notch from point number one. Borg took the first set with one break of serve, six games to four. But as would be the case all day, Gerulaitis would never give up and he fought back to even the match at a set apiece by winning the second set with a break of his own, six games to three.

As the match went on and the stakes got higher, so did the level of play. Once again, one break was all that was needed for Borg to take the third set, 6-3, and as Vitas fought back he only needed one break to even the match by taking the fourth set at 6-3 as well. When it came down to the deciding final set, neither man would give an inch. Finally, with the light of day dwindling, Gerulaitis reached match point. In the course of their rally, Vitas had a relatively easy backhand, the kind he'd hit millions of times in the past, to win the match.

And then it happened...the pressure of the moment finally seemed to catch up with the flamboyant American and he hit the backhand long. As often seems to happen with a great champion, Borg seized the momentum and went on to take the three hour-plus match by the score of 6-4, 3-6, 6-3, 3-6, 8-6. Borg ultimately defeated Jimmy Connors in an incredible five-set final that paled in comparison only to his match with Gerulaitis. The tournament win was Bjorg's second of five consecutive Wimbledon titles. Yet the real winners in the 1977 Championships were the spectators who were lucky enough to witness the classic semi-final match between two of tennis's all-time competitors, Bjorn Borg and Vitas Gerulaitis.

A Battle of Titans

Monica Seles v. Steffi Graf

Tennis's 38th most incredible moment occurred at the French Open finals in 1992. Steffi Graf and Monica Seles are arguably two of the best women ever to play the game of tennis. And although Graf had already racked up ten career Grand Slam titles coming into the 1992 French Open, as compared to five for Seles, Monica was rated the favourite. Despite Graf's three and a half year reign on top of the women's tour, the Yugoslavian-turned-American Seles had eclipsed Steffi as the world's number one in March of 1991. Furthermore, Seles had won the last four Grand Slam events she entered and was vying for her third straight French title. But the second-seeded Graf did have a couple of things in her favour. She had her huge forehand, and a partisan Parisian crowd chanting 'Steff-ee, Steff-ee' throughout the match. But despite Graf's considerable talent and crowd support, as the match got underway she was no match for the powerful Seles who was hitting her two-handed forehands and backhands with pinpoint accuracy. Before the athletic Graf knew what had hit her, Seles had captured the first set, six games to two, in just 26 minutes. But Graf didn't win a career 22 Grand Slam titles by giving up easily. As her forehand began to find its mark Steffi evened up the match by taking the second set 6-3.

As the grey skies began to brighten and the crowd grew enthralled, the match would come down to one set for all the marbles. The third set started with both women holding serve, but it would be Seles who drew first blood by breaking Graf to go up 2-1. The two combatants then continued to hold serve until Seles was leading five games to three and poised to take the championship. With Graf serving to stay alive, Seles found herself with a championship point, then a second, a third and finally a fourth, but each time Graf fought them off with her legendary steely resolve. After Graf eventually held serve the discouraged Seles lost her own serve at 15 and the score was even at 5-all.

As the match continued, the chants for the underdog Graf got louder and louder. With no tiebreakers in the final set at the French Open, both women went on to hold serve at 6-all and then again at 7-all. In the following game when Graf missed an easy forehand Seles went up eight games to seven and was serving for the title. Once again Graf stared down defeat as she broke back to even the now-epic match at eight games apiece. It was now gut-check time for Seles and she responded by breaking right back to go up 9-8. This time Seles' serve held strong and she quickly went up 40-15 to reach two more championship points. Graf held off her fifth match point with another huge forehand.

And then it happened...Graf had tempted fate once too often and on match point number six she made her 66th unforced error. Suddenly it was over. Seles had triumphed in an epic struggle, 6-2, 3-6, 10-8. Monica Seles had clearly established herself as the best woman on the planet and was poised to possibly go down as the best of all time.

And then it happened...See incredible moment #4.

Never Say Die

Wilmar Allison v. Giorgio de Stefani

Tennis's 37th most incredible moment occurred in a Davis Cup tie in 1931. Wilmar Lawson Allison was born on 8 December 1904 in San Antonio, Texas. Allison, a 5′ 11″, 155-pound (70-kilo) right-hander, came to prominence in 1927 when he captured the intercollegiate tennis title for the University of Texas. Although Allison had a stellar singles career which saw him ranked in the US top ten for eight consecutive years and win the 1935 US Singles Championship, he was best known for his outstanding doubles career with his long-time partner Johnny Van Ryn. Allison and Van Ryn won many doubles titles including the US Championships in 1931 and 1935, and the Wimbledon titles in 1929 and 1930. But the duo made their most prolific mark while playing for their country in Davis Cup competition. Their doubles record of 14-2 stood as the benchmark of Davis Cup doubles excellence for half a century until it was finally bested by arguably the best doubles team of all-time, John McEnroe and Peter Fleming, who posted a 14-1 record for the USA. Yet despite his doubles greatness Allison is remembered in tennis's 37th most incredible moment for a monumental singles effort.

The year was 1931 and Allison was to play the opening singles match for the United States in their semi-final Davis Cup tie with Italy's Giorgio de Stefani, a rare ambidextrous player. As the all-important first match got underway, Stefani seized the early advantage by taking the first set six games to four. Allison fought back and was poised to even the match at a set apiece on the four occasions of which he held set point. But Stefani staved off each of the four crucial points and took a commanding lead by winning the second set 9-7. Yet Allison was not to become a future Hall of Famer by giving up easily. After he won the third set 6-4 many thought the tide may be turning. However when Stefani went ahead 5-2 in the fourth set and eventually held two match points, it appeared to be curtains for the Texan. But once again Allison fought back and finally evened the match at two sets all by winning the set 8-6. It all came down to the fifth and final set. The match's earlier pattern then repeated itself when the Italian jumped out to another seemingly overwhelming lead, this time by the score of five games to one. But as the old adage goes, those who don't learn from history...

And then it happened...Stefani held a third match point, and then a fourth, and then a fifth, and on and on it went until, inconceivably, Allison held off a mind boggling *18* match points before finally prevailing, 4-6, 7-9, 6-4, 8-6, 10-8. Ironically, just one year later Jean Borotra of France turned the tables on Allison by saving four match points and defeating him, and consequently the United States, to capture the Davis Cup. I guess what they say is true, 'What goes around really does come around!'

The Dominator In White

Helen Wills Moody v. Helen Jacobs

Tennis's 36th most incredible moment occurred at the 1933 US Championship final. Helen Wills Moody was born on 6 October 1905 in California, and would become one of the all-time greats in tennis history. A steady, powerful baseliner, typically dressed in her conservative tennis whites (all the way down to her white eye shadow) Moody was known as 'Little Miss Poker Face' because of her stone-faced demeanour on the court. Because she didn't have the fashion sense of Gussy Moran or the flamboyance of Susan Lenglen, Moody won't be remembered specifically because of these traits. She simply won. And not only did she win an extraordinary 52 of 92 tournaments between 1919 and 1938, but her winning percentage was even more prolific when it counted the most...during the Grand Slams events.

The saga of this incredible 'moment' started in 1927 when Moody began the year on fire. She won match after match in a season that would see her win her first Wimbledon title and her fourth US Championship. In fact she went through the whole *year* without losing a single set! Not too shabby, but if you think that's impressive then you're going to love this. Moody ended up winning match after match, set after set in the most dominant fashion ever seen in the history of the game. Believe it or not, Moody went from 1927 through 1932 winning all 13 Grand Slams singles events she entered. As a matter of fact she won every match she played throughout the five-year span. And get this, she did it without dropping a single set! Moody would eventually win an unfathomable 158 matches in a row, encompassing 27 tournaments.

And then it happened...playing in the 1933 US singles final at Forest Hills, New York, Moody was forced to default in the third set for her only loss in 11 career match-ups to American Helen Jacobs. That ended the incredible streak, but Helen Wills Moody would ultimately complete her career with 19 Grand Slam singles titles out of a total of 22 Grand Slam tournaments entered. Considering that she compiled a Grand Slam singles match record of 126 wins and only three losses, all coming in finals, she is arguably the greatest Grand Slam champion of all time. Fittingly, many years after her brilliant reign had ended, Moody finally gave us one more thrill when she graced our sport by entering the International Tennis Hall of Fame in 1969.

Herr Wunderkind

Boris Becker v. Kevin Curren

Tennis's 35th most incredible moment occurred in the 1985 Wimbledon final. Although this match actually occurred on one Sunday afternoon, it was really a two-week coming out party for a then unknown 17-year-old teenager named Boris Becker. Boris Becker? Unknown you may be asking? Well, the man who went on to win six Grand Slam titles in his career was made a 100-1 long shot by the Ladbrokes bookmakers before the tournament began. But Boris would not remain inconspicuous for long. The Championships began smoothly enough for Becker with routine wins over Hank Pfister and Matt Anger. In a third-round match-up with the seventh-seeded Swede Joakim Nystrom, things really began to get interesting. It seemed that Nystrom had Becker ready for the kill on two separate occasions when he served for the match at 5-4 and again at 6-5 in the fifth set. But the unseeded Becker, who would show nerves of steel throughout the whole tournament, broke back both times and eventually won the match 9-7 in the final set.

At this point 'Boom Boom', a nickname Becker disliked due to its militaristic World War II connotations, didn't have long to wait until his next close call. In the very next round Becker's opponent was the Massachusetts native Tim Mayotte. Mayotte, whose game was perfectly suited to the fast grass courts of Wimbledon, was a particularly dangerous foe. Things became desperate for Becker when, with the score at 5 games all, serving at 30-40, and down two sets to one, he twisted his ankle. Although the rules allow only a 3-minute injury time out, 'Gentleman Tim' Mayotte didn't object when Becker needed five minutes to recover. Consequently, Boris was able to fight his way out of trouble and win the fourth set in a tiebreaker and then go on to win the match 6-2 in the fifth. As Becker went on to defeat the Frenchman Henri Leconte in the quarters and the fifth-seeded Anders Jarryd in the semis, he was on the verge of pulling off the triple feat: becoming not only the first German champion and the youngest champion, but also the first unseeded champion in the history of Wimbledon.

Becker's opponent in the final was the eighth-seeded South African-turned-American Kevin Curren. Curren was arguably playing the best tennis of his life, having routed defending champion John McEnroe in the quarters and Jimmy Connors in the semis. But it seemed as if not even the slightly favoured Curren could interfere with what appeared to be destiny.

And then it happened...after three hours and 18 minutes, with Becker up two sets to one and serving at 5-4, 40-30, Boom Boom served yet another one of his overpowering service winners to take the title 6-3, 6-7, 7-6, 6-4. Although Boris Becker would go on to become the biggest sports star in German history and one of the all-time great legends in our sport, let us not forget that it all started in 1985 when a little known man-child came out of nowhere to win the biggest tournament in tennis... Wimbledon!

The First to Win Them All

Fred Perry

Tennis's 34th most incredible moment occurred in 1935. Frederick John Perry was born on 18 May 1909 in Stockport, and would grow up to become Great Britain's greatest champion ever. Remarkably Perry, who was at first a table tennis champion, didn't pick up the game of tennis until the age of 18. But Fred was a quick learner and after he mastered his forehand, which had been his Achilles heel, there was no stopping him. Perry won his first Grand Slam singles title at the US Championships in 1933 by defeating Jack Crawford in the final. He followed up his 1933 Grand Slam by becoming only the second man to win three Grand Slam singles tournaments in a calendar year by defending his US Championship crown and by securing his first Australian and Wimbledon titles. Yet despite this success Perry must have felt a twinge of regret as he was denied the French Championship title, and consequently the label as the first ever 'Grand Slam champion' (this honour would go to Don Budge in 1938, see incredible moment #13), when he was beaten in the quarter-finals at Roland Garros by Italy's Giorgio de Stefani.

In 1935 Perry would not only have his revenge but also make history in the process. After his devastating loss to Stefani in 1934, Perry was quoted as saying, 'I told Giorgio after he beat me in Paris that I wouldn't allow him a game the next time.' Incredibly, Perry proved to be a man of his word. When he met Stefani again, this time in the Australian Championship quarter-finals in 1935, Perry thrashed the ambidextrous Italian (who had two forehands) with three love sets. That's right, Perry avenged his loss with a 6-0, 6-0, 6-0 drubbing. But the Englishman's work for the year of 1935 was not done. Perry was now vying to win the only Grand Slam tournament that eluded him, the French Championship. As he cruised into the semi-finals, his opponent was Jack Crawford. Crawford was no easy foe considering he had beaten Perry in the Australian final earlier in the year and had reached an incredible eight consecutive Grand Slam finals. But on this day Perry proved to be too good and dismissed Crawford in straight sets 6-3, 8-6, 6-3. Things would not get easier in the finals as Perry tried to make history. His opponent was the talented defending champion from Germany, Gottfried von Cramm. Perry started off strong, winning the first set 6-3. Von Cramm then fought back to even the match by taking the second set by the identical score of 6-3. But it seemed that on this day history would not be denied.

And then it happened...Perry won the final two sets and the match, 6-3, 3-6, 6-1, 6-3, and in doing so became the first man to win all four Grand Slam events. Frederick John Perry would eventually compile eight Grand Slam singles titles in his Hall of Fame career.

But none was as important or historic as his victory in 1935 when he won the French Championships and put himself right into the record books.

Let the Chaos Ensue

John McEnroe v. Ille Natase

Tennis's 33rd most incredible moment occurred at the 1979 US Open. It involved a cocky 19-year-old by the name of John McEnroe who was trying to make a name for himself, and a 33-year-old loudmouth by the name of Ille Nastase who was desperate for one last hurrah. As the night-time match began under the lights at Flushing Meadows, McEnroe came out fearlessly and took the first set, six games to four. But the old master Nastase, who had won the Open seven years earlier, had a few tricks up his sleeve and evened the match by taking the second set by the same score as the first. The brash Johnny Mac shot back by taking the third set 6-3, and now had a commanding two sets to one lead. To make things worse for the ageing Nastase, he would now have to go five sets if he wanted to advance to the third round.

The notorious Nastase may have been many things throughout his Hall of Fame career, but one thing he wasn't was stupid. Aware that he was in no shape to go five sets if the torrid pace continued, he began to stall despite the fact that he had been warned previously in the match for just such an infraction. After receiving a point penalty, things really began to get out of control as Nastase continued to soak up time. Consequently, the colourful chair umpire, Frank Hammond, had no alternative but to penalise Nastase a game, which put McEnroe up three games to one in the fourth set. Well, that was all Nastase and the boozed-up New York crowd needed to hear. As Nastase began to throw one of his patented tantrums, the raucous crowd showed their disapproval by heaving bottles, cans and basically anything they could get their hands on, onto the court. Despite the pleadings by Hammond to play on, Nastase took advantage of the fracas by continuing his diabolical behaviour. Eventually the referee, Mike Blanchard, instructed Hammond to strictly enforce the time regulations. When Nastase wouldn't budge, Hammond uttered the infamous words, 'Default Nastase. Game, Set, Match, McEnroe.'

Hammond's decision to default Nastase put the crowd into an absolute frenzy. This brought out the tournament director, Bill Talbert.

And then it happened... After 18 minutes of chaos, Talbert, sensing that the angry mob might trash the stadium, made a precedent-setting decision to reinstate Nastase after he had already been defaulted. And surprisingly, he removed Hammond from the chair, replacing him with Blanchard. At that point, both Nastase and the crowd calmed down enough to resume play. Ultimately, justice prevailed as McEnroe closed out the match in four quick games to complete one of the strangest contests in the annals of the US Open. As a follow-up, McEnroe would continue to make history when he defeated fellow New Yorker Vitas Gerulaitis in the finals for the first of his four US Open singles titles.

Court Justice

Stan Smith v. Ion Tiriac

Tennis's 32nd most incredible moment occurred in the 1972 Davis Cup final. After the United States had defeated Romania by the score of 5-0 in 1969 and 3-2 in 1971, the two countries would meet for a third time for the Cup in 1972. Although the finals were scheduled to be played on American soil, Ion Tiriac of Romania pleaded with USTA President Robert Colwell that this year's final should be played in Romania due to the fact that the previous two final encounters between the countries were played in the US. As it turned out, Colwell agreed. The incensed American crew, flabbergasted that such a decision could be made, coupled with the fact that there were death threats against Solomon and Gottfried, who were both Jewish, seriously contemplated boycotting the event in protest. But after team captain Dennis Ralston sold the US team on an 'us versus the world' mentality, the Americans flew to Bucharest for the finals.

The match was played at the Progresul Sports Club on slow red clay that heavily favoured the Romanians. Things now looked so bleak for the US team that Romania's Ille Nastase was quoted as saying, 'We cannot lose at home'. And as if the US didn't have enough adversity already, they would have to contend with a rambunctious, partisan Romanian crowd and, if you can believe this, corrupt hometown officials. The officiating actually became so egregious that the normally diplomatic Arthur Ashe charged that 'cheating by local officials reached an abysmal low.' But as they say, sometimes when you're given lemons you have to try to make lemonade.

As the first match got underway, Stan Smith of the US was pitted against Romania's Ille Nastase. Although Nastase was a heavy favourite on the red clay, he ultimately felt the heavy pressure and fell to Smith 11-9, 6-2, 6-3. Now with the US up one match to love, Ion Tiriac knew he had to defeat Tom Gorman for his country to have any chance of victory. With Gorman leading two sets to love, things looked dismal for the Romanians. But the tide started to turn when the already vocal crowd decided to really get involved. Consequently, whenever Gorman was to serve, hit a ground stroke, or needed to concentrate in the least bit, the spectators began to cough, clear their throats, or in some way make themselves a nuisance in general. Couple this with some controversial calls by the local linesmen and the result was a come-from-behind five-set victory for Tiriac.

The contest was now tied at a match apiece. After the US easily took the doubles it appeared as if the Davis Cup tie would come down to the Tiriac-Smith match-up since almost everyone assumed Nastase would easily defeat Gorman in the fifth and final match. As Smith and Tiriac began to do battle, things really starting getting ugly. The biased officials were giving every call possible to Tiriac. It got so bad that Smith was playing every ball that was less than a foot outside the lines. Furthermore, Smith's big serves were partly nullified by the numerous bogus foot-fault calls. Despite the adversity, Smith continued to fight gallantly, and as the match grew more intense, Tiriac began to cramp.

And then it happened...one of the 'non-partisan' local officials actually began massaging Tiriac's cramping leg! Yet incredibly, as the match got pushed into a fifth and deciding set, Smith displayed a champion's fortitude by winning 25 of the final 33 points, ultimately taking the final set at love. The US team had done it! They had won the Davis Cup under the most difficult of circumstances. Although

Nastase would go on to defeat Gorman in the now inconsequential fifth match to make the final score 3-2, it did not change the fact that the 1972 United States Davis Cup team had accomplished what few tennis fans thought they could. They ventured into a hostile territory, fighting the crowd, the officials and a very tough Romanian team, and pulled off one of the most unlikely victories in Davis Cup history.

Breaking the Colour Barrier

Althea Gibson v. Barbara Knapp

Tennis's 31st most incredible moment technically occurred at the 1950 US Championships, but in reality it was a lifetime in the making. This tale began on 25 August 1927 when a daughter was born to a poor black farming family in South Carolina. This baby's name was Althea Gibson. This tiny infant would soon grow up to be a tennis pioneer who would help pave the way for minorities in sports, as well as in American society, for generations to come. But this illustrious journey did not come without hitting lots of potholes.

When Althea was three years old her family moved north to Harlem. The family encountered overwhelming difficulty while living in New York during the Great Depression and began receiving welfare benefits. Furthermore, Althea was having her own troubles. She skipped school often, and her care ultimately came under the auspices of the Society for Prevention of Cruelty to Children. Yet despite her troubles, Althea was excelling in sports. She was often seen playing basketball with the boys of the area, shooting pool in the local pool halls or playing paddleball, which at the time was her best sport. Yet it was during a simple game of ping-pong that Althea's Hall of Fame tennis career was set into motion. While she was batting that little white ball back and forth across the table, the musician Buddy Walker noticed Althea's talent for the game and suggested that she might want to give tennis a try.

Althea began taking lessons at the Harlem Cosmopolitan Tennis Club and excelled almost immediately. As her abilities blossomed, she started entering, and winning, tennis tournaments throughout the state. At that time these tournaments were for African-American players only, but things were about to change. With talent, courage, and perseverance, Gibson racked up one tournament victory after another, and it became evident to many that she was not only the best black player of the land, but perhaps one of the best players period. Then, the former Wimbledon champion Alice Marble wrote an article for the *American Lawn Tennis* magazine. In her article, Marble stated in essence that the only reason one of the greatest players of the time was not allowed to participate in the major tournaments was due to pure, unadulterated bigotry. Gibson, who was currently enrolled as a university student became the first black player, male or female, to be entered into the national grass court championships at Forest Hills (today's US Open).

And then it happened...On 28 August 1950, on court number 14, Althea Gibson made history by defeating Barbara Knapp of England 6-2, 6-2. Gibson had broken the colour barrier! And although she lost a tension-filled second-round match to third-seeded Louise Brough 1-6, 6-3, 9-7, breaking the tennis colour barrier was just the first in a long list of firsts for the 5′ 11″ powerhouse. In 1956 Gibson would become the first African-American to win a Grand Slam event by defeating Angela Mortimer, 6-0, 12-10 to win the French Championships. She would follow that up by becoming the first black tennis player to win both the US Championships and Wimbledon in 1957, and she repeated the amazing double by doing it again in 1958. Due to her tennis dominance during these two magical years, Gibson became the first black athlete to win the Associated Press award for the 'Female Athlete of the Year' (she won the award in 1957 and 1958).

Gibson would eventually go on to win 11 Grand Slam titles in singles, doubles and mixed doubles combined. But tennis was not her only talent. She also went on to release a record album, *Althea Gibson Sings*, tour with the Harlem Globetrotters, play professional golf for several years (and actually win a tournament), and appear in several films. Although Gibson was named the 30th greatest female athlete of the twentieth

Who Said Grass Is Only for Cows?

Martina Navratilova v. Zina Garrison

Tennis's 30th most incredible moment occurred at the 1990 Wimbledon Ladies Final. Martina Navratilova and Wimbledon go together like bacon and eggs but it wasn't always that way. Born on 18 October 1956 in Prague (in then Czechoslovakia), Martina learned to play tennis on the slow clay courts of Eastern Europe. Unbelievably, when the woman who is considered to be the greatest fast-court player of all time first came to Wimbledon in 1973, she had never set foot on a grass court until a week before her first Wimbledon match. Yet Navratilova's aggressive serve and volley style was perfectly suited for the speedy grass of Wimbledon and she eventually took her first title at the All England Club in 1978 by defeating the top-seeded Chris Evert. (Beating Evert in the Wimbledon finals would prove habit forming as Navratilova would end their rivalry by holding a 5-0 Wimbledon finals record over her friend and tennis foe.)

After losing in the semi-finals in 1980 and 1981, Navratilova would go on to win six straight Wimbledon singles titles between 1982 and 1987, to break the great Suzanne Lenglen's record of five successive Wimbledon victories between 1919 and 1923. This also tied Helen Wills Moody's all time mark of eight Wimbledon singles titles. Now, at the ancient tennis age of 33, Martina was once again trying to make Wimbledon history. Luckily for Martina, Zina Garrison was helping her with some of the groundwork. Garrison held off a match point in the quarter-finals to defeat Monica Seles and then went on to defeat Steffi Graf, Navratilova's Achilles heel of the last two years, in the semis. And even though Garrison, at age 26, was playing the best tennis of her life, Martina had to feel confident with the knowledge that she had beaten Garrison 27 times out of their 28 previous meetings.

As the two women walked on to Centre Court, they were both vying for history. Navratilova was looking for her record-breaking ninth Wimbledon title, and Garrison was attempting to become the first African-American woman to win a tennis major since Althea Gibson in 1958. (See incredible moment #31.) But on this day it appeared as if Navratilova was on a mission.

And then it happened...Martina played some of her most inspired tennis in years. She hit 32 winners and committed only nine unforced errors as she cruised to a 6-4, 6-1 victory. Although Navratilova would reach one more Wimbledon final, in 1994, a tenth title was not in the cards as she lost to Conchita Martinez in three sets. Yet when it was all said and done, Navratilova had won the most Wimbledon singles titles in history with a total of nine. She had the most Wimbledon singles victories with 119. She reached the most consecutive Wimbledon singles finals with nine in a row, and ended her career with an astonishing Wimbledon singles record of 119 wins to only 13 losses. In Martina's Hall of Fame career, she also amassed three Australian Open singles titles, two French Open singles titles, four US Open singles titles and a plethora of Grand Slam doubles and mixed doubles titles to boot. Yet Martina Navratilova will always be remembered first and foremost as being the greatest Wimbledon Champion ever to play the game.

Little Mo

Maureen Connolly

Tennis's 29th most incredible moment occurred in 1953. Maureen Catherine Connolly was born on 17 September 1934. A tennis prodigy like few others, she was aptly nicknamed 'Little Mo', a name derived from the USS *Missouri* which was a battleship with the nickname of 'Big Mo'. After a shaky start that saw her lose in the second round in her first two attempts at the US Championships at Forest Hills, Little Mo's career took off. But when she won the US titles in 1951 and 1952 and Wimbledon in 1952, she was poised to accomplish one of the greatest achievements in the history of tennis. 1953 started with Connolly easily defeating her doubles partner, Julie Sampson, in the finals of the Australian Championships 6-3, 6-2. It was then on to the French Championships where she took the title with a triumph over Hart 6-2, 6-4. Hart again fell victim to Little Mo's greatness in a hard-fought Wimbledon final by the score of 8-6, 7-5. As Connolly travelled to the US Championships she was vying to become the first woman to win the coveted Grand Slam of tennis, and only the second player ever to do so. (Don Budge won tennis's first Grand Slam 15 years earlier in 1938 – see incredible moment #13.) Yet neither the pressure of the moment nor the other talented players would stand in the way of history. For the third straight Grand Slam final Connolly once again faced Hart.

And then it happened...Little Mo finished off Hart 6-2, 6-4 to win the

US Singles Championship for the third straight year, and in doing so became an immortal by winning the Grand Slam. And as if her greatness had not already been established, Little Mo would finish the year with a 61 win and one loss record and would eventually win the next nine majors that she entered. (One Australian Championship, two French Championships, three Wimbledon Championships, and three US Championship titles.) Sadly, despite her greatness, fate had a different plan for Little Mo. In 1954 she suffered a career-ending leg injury as a result of a horse-riding accident. Then, after teaching tennis for several years, Connolly would tragically die of cancer in 1969 at the all-too-young age of 34.

Although the duration of Maureen 'Little Mo' Connolly's career was only a fraction of a typical player's, she was as bright a star as any, before or since. And to this very day 'Little Mo' is still considered to be one of the greatest players in the history of the sport.

Mr. Sandman

Goran Ivanisevic v. Patrick Rafter

Tennis's 28th most incredible moment occurred at the 2001 Wimbledon final. For Goran Ivanisevic, this year's tournament represented the chance for a storybook ending to a nightmarish journey. The 29-year-old Croat was desperate to win the Grand Slam that he coveted more than any other. Having been a three-time bridesmaid, losing in the 1992 finals to Andre Agassi (see incredible moment #57), and in 1994 and 1998 to Pete Sampras, Goran had been so close and yet so far. To make matters worse, Ivanisevic had been one of the world's best players, reaching a career-high ranking of number 2 in 1995, only to see his standing plummet in the previous year and a half to an abysmal number 125 at the beginning of the Wimbledon fortnight. After coming off an embarrassing 6-1, 6-1 defeat at the Queen's Club tournament, a Wimbledon tune-up, things were so bad for Ivanisevic that the Wimbledon committee had to grant him a wild-card entry just to qualify for the tournament. Under these circumstances, just about everyone and their mothers had given Ivanisevic about the same chance of winning Wimbledon as John McEnroe has of winning a self-control contest. But, as they say, 'That's why they play the tournament.'

As fate would have it, Goran won his first match, then the next, and the next, until once again he found himself in the final. But this time he would face a new foe, that of last year's runner-up and third-seeded

Australian, Patrick Rafter. Due to a rainy Sunday the final was postponed until Monday for the first time since 1922. The Wimbledon final is normally sold out months in advance, but thanks to the rain gods 10,000 tickets were sold in the two and a half hours preceding the match. The result was a young, raucous crowd, more typical of a rock concert than a serious event like a Wimbledon final. Throughout the match the animated crowd cheered, ooh'd and ah'd, and roared with delight as the players put on one of the best Wimbledon finals ever played. The seesaw match saw the momentum swing back and forth, and back again. Ivanisevic jumped out to an early lead when he won the first set 6-3. Rafter fought back to take the second by the same 6-3 score. Now it was Goran's turn to step up to the plate, and he did so by winning the third set, again at 6-3, to take a two sets to one advantage. To this point in the match, the volatile Croat had been uncharacteristically able to keep his emotions in check...until now. As Goran served at break point in the fourth set he hit a service winner, but when the lineswoman called a foot fault Ivanisevic yelled out in agony. Things went from bad to worse when an apparent second serve ace was called wide, giving Rafter a crucial break of serve. As Goran threw his racquet, kicked the net and argued with the chair umpire, it looked like more of the same from one of the most talented players never to win a major. And when Rafter ran out the set 6-2 to even the match at two sets all, many thought they saw the door of opportunity closing on Goran for the final time. But Ivanisevic, knowing that this was perhaps his last chance at Wimbledon glory, was able to compose himself for the fifth and final set that would determine the champion.

As both men tenaciously held their serves and the score remained even, the tension became almost unbearable. When Goran served at 6-7, love-30, he was only two points from defeat. But as he had done during the entire tournament, Goran relied on his big lefty serve to bail him out of trouble, and he levelled the set at seven games all. As so often happens in sports, after flirting with the brink of defeat, Ivanisevic was able to regain the momentum by pulling off a service break of his own in the very next game. As he came out to serve for the championship at 8-7, it looked as if he just might pull off one of the greatest feats in the history of tennis. For up until this point, no man or woman wild-card entry had ever gone on to win a Grand Slam championship title. Yet when Ivanisevic reached 40-30, he was on the verge of making history.

And then it happened...as Goran attempted to win what is considered the to be the toughest point in tennis – the final point – he hit his second serve five feet long to double fault. Then, at the second championship point he double faulted again! After squandering his third match point, it looked like he may have been tempting fate one too many times. But finally, almost mercifully, after three hours of gruelling tennis, on championship point number four Goran's big serve finally bailed him out. A service winner gave him the title that he had waited a lifetime to achieve, the Championships of Wimbledon. After the elated victor fell to the court in tears and climbed into the stands to hug his father, family and friends, he was quoted as saying, 'I don't know if it's a dream or not. I'm afraid somebody will wake me up and say I didn't win Wimbledon again.' Well you can rest assured, Goran, for you are now, and will always be, a Wimbledon champion!

The Rocket

Rod Laver

Tennis's 27th most incredible moment occurred in 1969. Rodney George Laver was born on 9 August 1939. Coincidentally, that was just a month before the great Don Budge would make history by becoming the first player to accomplish tennis's greatest feat, the calendar Grand Slam. (That's what we writers like to call *'foreshadowing'.*) As a small, sickly child, 'The Rocket', as Laver would come to be known, looked nothing like a future tennis superstar. Yet despite the fact that Rod only grew to become 5' 8" and 145 pounds (65 kilos), he actually developed great strength and power. In fact, his left arm would become legendary for its disproportionately large size. When measured it was found to be larger than that of the boxing champion, Rocky Marciano. Rod began to win match after match and tournament after tournament. Then, in 1962, Rod 'Rocket' Laver had a year of greatness. After defeating Roy Emerson for the Australian and French Championship titles, he went on to claim the Wimbledon crown, overwhelming Marty Mulligan in the finals. And when Laver met Emerson once again, this time in the US Championship finals, he was ready to make history.

And then it happened... Laver defeated Emerson to become only the second man, and the third player in history, to win tennis's Grand Slam. But hold on to your hats, because the Australian great had more in store for us. After turning professional at the end of his historic 1962 season, Laver fought it out in the professional ranks against the likes of Pancho Gonzalez and Ken Rosewall. Then, in 1968, a historic event occurred. Tennis ushered in the 'Open Era' and 'opened up' its doors to all players, amateur and professional alike. Consequently Laver, and all of the other professionals, was given another Grand Slam life. And the Rocket would prove to make the most of it! After winning the Wimbledon Singles Championship for the third time in 1968, Rod had his sights set on 1969. In the year's first Grand Slam at the Australian Open, The Rocket was severely tested in the semi-finals against fellow Australian Tony Roche. On a day where the temperature reached 105 degrees the two mates fought it out for over four hours until Laver finally came out on top 7-5, 22-20, 9-11, 1-6, 6-3. After his gruelling semi-final, the final must have seemed like a breeze as Laver easily ousted Andres Gimeno in straight sets for the title.

It was then on to the French Open, where another fellow Australian, Dick Crealy, would test Laver once again. In the second round Crealy took the first two sets, only to see Rod come back to win in five. From that point it was smooth sailing as Laver would drop only two more sets in his next four matches, taking the title by punishing the great Ken Rosewall in straight sets. It was then a quick hop, skip and jump over to Wimbledon where Laver once again found second-round trouble, this time to the little-known Indian named Premjit Lall. But after losing the first two sets, Laver would come back to secure a five-set victory. After another five-set win, this time over the American Stan Smith in the fourth round, Laver raced through the rest of the field and found victory once again when he up-ended John Newcombe in a four-set final. Laver was now on the verge of setting a standard of excellence that may never be duplicated. The Rocket won his first three US Open matches in straight sets, but would find trouble in the fourth round when he had to come back from two sets to one down to defeat Dennis Ralston. After dismissing Emerson in the quarters and Ashe in the semis, Laver was poised for unprecedented territory. On a gloomy, overcast day, Laver lost the first set to Roche 7-9. He then bounced back, taking the next two sets 6-1, 6-2, and was now only one set away.

Wager the Triple

Bobby Riggs

Tennis's 26th most incredible moment occurred at Wimbledon in 1939. Robert Larimore Riggs was born on 25 February 1918 in Los Angeles, California. Because Riggs was slight in stature and short in height, he lacked the power of many of his contemporaries but made up for it with cunning, grit and a somewhat outrageously flamboyant personality. The master of the drop shot and lob, Riggs used brains over brawn to win many a match. Although Bobby will always be remembered most for his infamous battle of the sexes match with Billie Jean King in 1973 (see incredible tennis moment #3), it was 34 years earlier when Riggs first made tennis history. As the story goes, Riggs, always the hustler, was playing in his first Wimbledon in 1939 at the age of 21. In a typical display of audacity, Riggs went to a London bookmaker and bet $500 on himself to win the singles event. Yet it appeared that the 3-1 odds for the second-seeded Riggs were not enticing enough. He then asked for the odds of winning the doubles, and received 6 to 1. Undaunted, he then asked for odds for winning the mixed doubles and was given 12-1. Bobby, seeing green, brazenly decided to combine his bets to incorporate all three events. As Riggs later put it, 'I had to win all three or lose it all.'

Although no man had ever pulled off the Wimbledon triple, Riggs jumped in with both feet and began fighting his way through all three draws. Things started off smoothly enough but Riggs' first scare came in the doubles quarter-finals. Partnered with Elwood Cooke, Riggs found his team down two sets to one before prevailing 11-9 in the fifth. Riggs and Cooke cruised from there, winning the final in four sets and thereby achieving the first leg of the triple. Riggs' partner in the mixed doubles was fellow Californian Alice Marble, and the two compatriots were never seriously challenged as they cruised through the draw and defeated Britain's team of Brown and Wilde 9-7, 6-1 for the title.

Riggs was now two thirds of the way home but his most perilous battle was yet to come. His next opponent was Elwood Cooke, his doubles partner, in the singles final. Riggs lost the first set 6-2 but fought back to take the second, 8-6, and level the match. When Cooke captured the third set 6-3 to take a two sets to one advantage, Riggs would later say, 'When I was down two to one in sets I thought about my investment.' That incentive may have been exactly what Riggs needed.

And then it happened...Riggs came from behind once again to win the deciding two sets and the Championship, 2-6, 8-6, 3-6, 6-3, 6-2. Riggs had done it! He had become the first and only man to pull off the Wimbledon triple crown by winning the singles, doubles and mixed doubles championships in the same year. Remarkably, this was the only year Riggs ever played in the Wimbledon Championships and therefore left an unblemished Wimbledon legacy on his record.

And what about the pay-off? Because Riggs was playing as an amateur he was awarded the prestigious Wimbledon trophy, but nothing in the way of prize money for his victory. No need to shed tears for poor Bobby, however. By pulling off the historic triple in 1939, the 21-year-old hustler had leveraged his $500 investment into an astounding $108,000. From the wily Riggs' perspective, not a bad day at the office. Not bad at all!

Jack and the Bean Stalk

Jack Crawford v. Ellsworth Vines

Tennis's 25th most incredible moment occurred at the 1933 Wimbledon final. John Herbert Crawford, known to all simply as Jack, was one of the greatest champions of the first half of the twentieth century. Born on 22 March 1908 in Albury, Australia, Crawford was aptly nicknamed 'Gentleman Jack' for his tremendous sportsmanship. The 6' 1", 185-pound (82-kilo) right-hander played a classic game of tennis with textbook strokes, despite using an antiquated flat-headed racquet. Using his flawless style and prodigious talent he amassed 17 Grand Slam titles and was inducted into the International Tennis Hall of Fame in 1979. Crawford's impressive record speaks for itself, yet there was one match that defined his career, the 1933 Wimbledon final versus Californian Ellsworth Vines.

Coming into the 1933 Wimbledon Championships, Crawford had already secured the three previous Australian Championships and the French Championship played months earlier, but was still looking for his first title at the Big 'W'. Throughout the tournament, his opponent Vines had easily dismissed all comers as he made his way to the finals. Crawford's path was not as pristine, but after fighting off the game Frenchman Henri Cochet in a tough four-set battle he was on the brink of seizing his first Wimbledon title.

The major obstacle in the Australian's way was, of course, Ellsworth

Vines, the defending champion. London bookmakers had made Vines a heavy five-to-one favourite. As the finals got underway, Vines used his big serve to take the first set and the early lead, six games to four. In the second set Vines had two excellent chances to take control of the match as he had Crawford down love-40 on two separate occasions. But the determined Crawford fought his way out of trouble both times and eventually evened the match by winning the set 11-9. Using the momentum from the second set, Crawford peppered shot after shot to Vines' weaker backhand side to seize the third set and the advantage 6-2. Yet the momentum swung again, this time in Vines' favour, and he evened the match a second time by taking the fourth set 6-2. After two hours of exemplary play, the match and the title had come down to the fifth and final set.

As they began by holding serve, both players were vying for that one crucial break. Vines had a couple of early chances at two all and three all, but Crawford held him off. Then, with Crawford leading by five games to four and Vines serving, Crawford changed up his return strategy by moving well inside the baseline and merely blocking back Vines' huge serve. The strategy paid off in a big way as Crawford won the first point, then the second, and then the third to take a love-40, triple-match-point advantage.

And then it happened...as Crawford blocked back another rocket serve, the unnerved Vines put the final volley into the net and it was all over. John Herbert Crawford had won what was considered the best Wimbledon final ever to be played to date. As A. Wallis Myers, a sports journalist at the time, so eloquently put it, 'There have only been ten five-set finals in the history of the meeting. Today's, for superlative play, refined coordination of strokes and tactics, continuous speed in service and the fighting vigour of both men at the finish, must rank first.'

The Thrill of Victory and the Agony of Defeat

Ivan Lendl v. John McEnroe

Tennis's 24th most incredible moment occurred at the 1984 French Open Final. The contestants for this Grand Slam title were John McEnroe and Ivan Lendl, and the outcome would be one that would greatly shape the legacy of both men. For McEnroe's part, to date he had already won on the grass courts of Wimbledon twice and on the hard courts at the US Open three times. McEnroe was looking to become the first of his contemporaries to win three different Grand Slam titles on three different surfaces. (Borg never did win on the hard courts at the US Open, Connors never won on the red clay at Roland Garros, and Lendl never prevailed on the grass courts of Wimbledon.) In 1984, McEnroe was the number one player and was in his first, and what would be his only, French Open final, and wanted desperately to solidify his position as one of the greatest players in the history of the sport. To top it off, McEnroe was also vying to become the first American to win the French since Tony Trabert did so in 1954 and 1955. On the other hand, Lendl was looking to get off the 'schnide'. Lendl had been a Grand Slam finalist at the French Open in 1981, the US Open in 1982 and 1983, and at the Australian Open in 1983. The results of these efforts were four runner-up trophies. That's right, Lendl was zero for four, and he had been given the label of a perennial choker who couldn't win the big one.

As the match got underway it looked as if Lendl was in for more of the same. Johnny Mac was completely dominant, sweeping the first two sets after conceding only ten points on serve. But although Mac's tennis may have been top notch, the same could not be said for his behaviour.

And then it happened... Inexplicably, at one game apiece in the third set, McEnroe began to lose his temper and, consequently, his focus. First, McEnroe was annoyed by a cameraman's headset making too much noise, and angrily let him know it. Soon thereafter McEnroe was yelling at photographers. As Lendl was fighting back from love-30 in one service game and from love-40 in the next, things started to, in McEnroe's words, 'snowball'. Lendl was eventually able to break McEnroe's serve and capture the third set, six games to four. McEnroe again had chances to pull away in the fourth. On two occasions he was up a break but couldn't back it up, giving the breaks back in his following service games and eventually losing the set at 5-7.

As the two men fought through the fifth set it was either man's for the taking. Then, when McEnroe couldn't convert on two more break points at 3-all in the fifth set, it appeared as if it was McEnroe, and not Lendl, who was nervously choking away the title. Finally, at championship point, as McEnroe pushed an easy forehand volley wide, Lendl threw his arms up in the air. Ivan Lendl had done it! After his fifth Grand Slam final, Lendl could finally call himself a Grand Slam champion. Apparently spurred on by the taste of sweet victory, Lendl would end his career with a total of eight Grand Slam titles in all. And although McEnroe would go on to win Wimbledon and the US Open later in the year, he never did win that elusive French Open. When the two great champions' professional playing days were finally over, Ivan Lendl would call this match his greatest triumph, whereas John McEnroe would call the loss the most painful of his career.

The Choke

Jana Novotna v. Steffi Graf

Tennis's 23rd most incredible moment occurred at the Wimbledon women's final in 1993. As the championships began, Jana Novotna, the 24-year-old eighth-seeded Czech, was seeking her first major title. Novotna, who was considered one of the best women on the WTA tour to never have won a Grand Slam, was desperate to net that elusive Grand Slam title. Furthermore, her aggressive attacking style of play made the fast grass courts of Wimbledon the perfect forum. Jana served and volleyed her way through the first five rounds of the tournament. Then in round six she looked to be in top form as she easily dispatched the number two seed and greatest Wimbledon champion of all time, Martina Navratilova, in straight sets in the semi-finals. Yet Novotna's biggest hurdle still remained before she could hoist the Venus Rosewater Dish, the golden sphere trophy given to the women's champion. Novotna's long-time nemesis, the number one seed and defending champion, Steffi Graf was waiting for Novotna in the finals.

Looming over Novotna like an ominous sky were some scary numbers. Specifically, '16' and '19'. That is to say that Graf had defeated Novotna in 16 of the 19 matches that they had played throughout their careers. Yet as the first set of the finals progressed, Novotna was matching Graf shot for shot. When the first set ended, however, it was Graf who came out on top of an excruciatingly tight tiebreaker, eight points to six. Novotna, sensing she was playing at the top of her game, would not give an inch. And incredibly, Novotna began doing the unthinkable. Jana was taking complete control of the match, winning the second set 6-1 and jumping out to a commanding four games to one, two service break lead in the third and deciding set. Playing flawlessly, Jana was poised to take the biggest tennis tournament in the world.

And then it happened...How can I say this tactfully? Well...she CHOKED! Novotna was serving at game point for a seemingly insurmountable five games to one lead when she double faulted. As one unforced error led to another, and then another, Graf, being the champion that she is, began to find her form. Then, as Novotna was serving at four games to three, she threw in three more double faults to donate yet another game. And in about the amount of time it takes to say 'collapse', Graf had rattled off five games in a row and was the Wimbledon champion once again.

Although the match may have ended, there was still more drama to come. In the time-honoured Wimbledon trophy ceremony, the Duchess of Kent was presenting the runner-up award to an emotionally frazzled Novotna. Attempting to console Jana, the sympathetic Duchess said, 'Don't worry Jana, I know you can do it.' Well, that was all Novotna needed to hear and the flood gates opened. Novotna broke down and the Duchess took Jana in her arms while Novotna wept on her shoulder. It was this heartfelt show of emotion that became the defining moment of the 1993 Wimbledon Championships. Yet lest you should despair for the plight of the fair maiden Czech, she would have her day in the sun. After losing to Martina Hingis in the 1997 Wimbledon final she would eventually prevail by defeating the Frenchwoman Nathalie Tauziat, to finally become a Wimbledon Champion in 1998.

Sister Act

Serena Williams v. Venus Williams

Tennis's 22nd most incredible moment occurred during the 2003 Australian Open, but this episode really started about 20 years earlier on the crime-ridden streets of Compton, California. As the legend goes, Richard Williams saw a women's tennis match on television where the winner received a rather large cheque, and he decided right then and there that he was going to have a couple of daughters and make them tennis champions. Considering that this was a financially disadvantaged African-American family, and that the world of tennis didn't exactly fit that socio-economic profile, Mr Williams's vision seemed more than a little farfetched. But from the time that young Venus and Serena could walk, father Richard was telling everyone who would listen that one day his daughters would be the top two players in the world, fighting it out for Grand Slam championships.

Fast forward to the 2001 US Open final, at which Richard appeared to be the ultimate prognosticator when big sister Venus defeated younger sister Serena 6-2, 6-4 to claim the title. And as incredible as this story is, the truly amazing part is still yet to come. In 2002, Venus and Serena met again in another Grand Slam final. It was the French Open and this time younger sister Serena came away with the straight set title 7-5, 6-3. And guess what...several weeks later the sisters met again in the Wimbledon final, and once again Serena defeated Venus in straight sets, this time by the score of 7-6, 6-3.

Now Serena was beginning to get on a roll. Whereas Venus had won five of the first six professional encounters between the two sisters, Serena had now won three in a row including the aforementioned last two Grand Slam titles. Additionally, Serena was now clearly playing the most dominant tennis in the world and was half way to completing a feat that had only been accomplished by four women previously...holding all four Grand Slam titles at the same time.

Technically, this was not the 'Grand Slam' as defined by holding all four titles in one calendar year, but the accomplishment was still seen as extraordinary. As Serena made her way to the 2002 US Open final she was met once again by who else but her big sister Venus. To add to the hype, the women's final was being shown by CBS in a prime-time slot on a Saturday night. But history was to repeat itself once again as little sister Serena was victorious by the score of 6-4, 6-3.

As the sisters came to the 2003 Australian Open, tennis journalists and fans alike were asking the same questions. Would Serena make history by winning her fourth major tournament in a row, and would the sisters meet in an unprecedented fourth straight Grand Slam final? It seemed as if all the hype would be for nothing as Serena struggled mightily in her first-round match against the Frenchwoman Emilie Loit. Ultimately she managed to survive by winning the final set, seven games to five, but this match seemed like a piece of cake compared to Serena's semi-final match against Belgium's Kim Clijsters. Serena trailed Clijsters 5-1 in the third, and at 5-2 she had to fight off two match points. In a storybook tournament that seemed like destiny, Serena was able to rally all the way back to beat Clijsters and set up a final match-up with none other but her sister Venus. In their six previous Grand Slam matches they had yet to have a match that went all three sets. Yet in this historic encounter things would be different. Serena won the first set in a tiebreaker, 7-6, but Venus found her serve and recouped to win the second, 6-3.

In the last set the sisters continued to give it their all. When Serena eventually took the lead, 5-4, she was only one game away from history. With all the pressure in the sports world focused solely on every point it was clear that someone had to crack.

And then it happened... Venus committed four errors and before you could say 'Serena Slam', history had been written. Serena joined Connolly, Court, Navratilova and Graf to become only the fifth woman to hold all four major titles at one time. And although tennis historians view Serena's 'Grand Slam' as inferior to Conolly's, Court's and Graf's because those three women won theirs in the same calendar year, the fact that Serena won hers in four finals against her sister Venus (who by the way became the first player to lose four straight Grand Slam finals), makes this Grand Slam one for the books. As Serena said herself, 'I am making history right now. It doesn't happen every day.'

I See You Had the Pasta for Lunch

Pete Sampras v. Alex Corretja

Tennis's 21st most incredible moment occurred at the 1996 US Open. Throughout 1996 Pete Sampras was the world's number one player, but despite this fact he had yet to win a major title. After failing at the Australian, French and Wimbledon, Pete was looking to capture his last remaining Grand Slam chance of the year, the US Open. As Sampras was cruising through the draw he had what most thought of as a quick stop off at the quarter-finals against the 31st ranked, 22-year-old Spaniard, Alex Corretja. Most tennis pundits saw Corretja as a clay court specialist who would provide scant resistance for the mighty three-time US Open Champion. But Corretja had other plans. From game one, Corretja was matching Sampras shot for shot. Playing on a hot and humid afternoon, Sampras won the first set, 7-6, but Corretja fought back to take the next two sets, 7-5, 7-5. The lengthy match was now being played under the night-time lights, and Pete didn't give an inch as he recovered to win the fourth set, 6-4. Despite the fact that Corretja had been outplaying Sampras for much of the match, the score was now tied at two sets apiece. But the great Pete Sampras, like all the Greek gods, had an Achilles heel.

For all of his greatness, Sampras had struggled with physical problems and injuries throughout his career. As the fifth set progressed, the exhausted Sampras was labouring. Finally, as they reached the decisive tiebreaker (the US Open is the only Grand Slam event to have a final set tiebreaker), Sampras looked as if he could be knocked over with a feather. The tiebreaker was tied at one point apiece.

And then it happened...as Sampras was hunched over at the back of the court a fan from the stadium yelled out, 'Pete Puked!' And sure enough, the extremely dehydrated, fatigued Sampras had vomited at the back of stadium court. After receiving a time violation warning from the chair umpire, the courageous Sampras fought on. Although Pete was hunched over in a combination of pain and exhaustion after every point of the tiebreaker, he eventually reached match point at six points to five. But when he sent a forehand long and lost the next point as well, Corretja had reached his first match point at seven points to six. Now Corretja hit a passing shot that looked like a clean winner and it appeared that he had achieved the biggest upset of his career. But Sampras, summoning up all the strength he could muster, lunged and hit a forehand volley for a winner. Then, at seven points all and a second serve on his racquet, Sampras hit a 90 mile an hour serve out wide for an ace! With the crowd in a complete frenzy, Corretja was serving at seven points to eight, but this time pressure was too much for Corretja to handle and he double-faulted to give Sampras the match, 7-6, 5-7, 5-7, 6-4, 7-6. In the longest match of the year's tournament (four hours and 9 minutes), Corretja had hit 90 winners and made only 30 unforced errors, compared with 74 winners and 68 unforced errors for Sampras. Pete had been outplayed statistically but somehow the great champion found a way to win. After the match, Sampras, who was given two litres of intravenous fluid, dedicated the effort to his late coach, Tim Gullikson. Today the match is remembered as one of the best to have ever been played at the US Open. And this from a man the press had once labelled as being boring!

Big Mac's Revenge

John McEnroe v. Bjorn Borg

Tennis's 20th most incredible moment occurred at the 1980 US Open. Bjorn Borg and John McEnroe had just come off arguably the best tennis match ever played to date in their epic 1980 Wimbledon Final. (See incredible moment #2.) And now, several months later at the US Open, the tennis world was frenzied at the thought of another Borg/McEnroe duel. Licking his chops at the chance for revenge, McEnroe had stated at the beginning of the tournament that if he were able to defend his US Open crown of 1979, there would no player he would rather defeat in the final than Bjorn Borg.

The dream final match-up looked to be in danger when both men had to default at the Canadian Open due to injuries just a couple of weeks prior to the Open. But come tournament time both men were ready to go, although they would encounter some bumps in the road. The two stars reached the quarter-finals rather comfortably, but they would both have to gut it out from there. First, Borg was down two sets to one and four games to two in the fourth set against American Roscoe Tanner, who had defeated him at the US Open the previous year. This year he was able to pull out a five-set victory.

On the other side of the draw, McEnroe was having his own difficulties with Ivan Lendl in their quarter-final encounter before Johnny Mac was able to prevail in four sets. It was then on to the semi-finals where Borg dropped the first two sets to talented South African Johan Kriek before coming back to win in five. And then there was McEnroe who was engulfed in an epic semi-final match against his long-time nemesis, Jimmy Connors. The two men played extraordinary tennis for more than four hours before McEnroe took the thriller in a fifth-set tiebreaker.

Now the dream final was set. Despite the fact that McEnroe's marathon semi-final left him with less than 24 hours to prepare for the finals, the fatigued American came out strong and took the first set in a tiebreaker. Carrying the momentum, he took the second set as well, 6-1. But it should have come as no surprise that Borg, who was renowned for coming back from two sets to love down, fought back to take the third set, 7-6.

After Bjorn took the gruelling fourth set, 7-5, an exhausted McEnroe would later say, 'I thought my body was going to fall off'. But with the memories of Wimbledon several months earlier swirling around in his head, McEnroe didn't let up. When he broke Bjorn's serve at 3-all in the deciding set he found a second wind and jumped out to a 5-4, 40-15 lead, match point.

And then it happened…McEnroe served, rushed the net, stuck a crisp volley into the open court, and the title was his once again. McEnroe would go on to avenge his Wimbledon loss the following year by defeating Borg in the 1981 Wimbledon finals, and later that year would turn him away once more at Flushing Meadows. In the aftermath of this series of Grand Slam losses to McEnroe, the great Bjorn Borg, who had once stated that he wanted to be remembered as the greatest tennis player who ever lived, walked away from the game at the age of 25.

Getting Your Money's Worth

Semi-Final Day at the US Open

Tennis's 19th most incredible moment occurred on 8 September 1984. When a Grand Slam tournament enters its final stages, it's like a great novel reaching its climax. You can't wait to see how it all turns out, but most likely have a twinge of regret that the excitement will soon be coming to an end. And as any tennis fan will tell you, this is most evident at the US Open.

Whereas most Grand Slam tournaments play the women's semi-finals on Thursday, the men's semi-finals on Friday, the women's finals on Saturday, and wrap things up with the men's final on Sunday, the US Open adds its own special twist. Typical of most American events, things are bigger and better at the Open. In a made-for-television extravaganza, the Open format features both men's semi-final matches and the women's final match all on one magical stage that has become known as 'Super Saturday'.

On a beautiful September day in 1984, Super Saturday lived up to its name...and then some. The first ball was struck at 11:07 am, in a two out of three set men's 35-and-over match between the former champion Stan Smith and the formidable Australian, John Newcombe. Smith prevailed in an entertaining three setter that would turn out to be only the first of several memorable encounters in a long but very special day. By the time Ivan Lendl and Pat Cash took the court for their semi-final match-up, the day was already behind schedule. And it appeared as if Lendl and Cash also forgot their watches as they embarked on an epic contest which stretched out for five long sets. For the spectators it was worth it, though, because in the midst of this protracted struggle, events reached a crescendo when Lendl, at match point down, hit a running forehand topspin lob that landed on the baseline for a clean winner. In this moment of high drama, Lendl had stared defeat in the face and laughed. Then, flushed with both relief and exultation, Ivan broke Cash's serve and carried the momentum to a thrilling 3-6, 6-3, 6-4, 6-7, 7-6 victory and a cherished spot in the finals.

Now it was time for the women to take centre stage, well behind schedule. But as the fans had come to expect, Chris Evert and Martina Navratilova often played spectacular matches, and this contest would be no exception. After Evert jumped out to a 6-4 lead, Navratilova battled back to take the second set and tie the match at a set apiece. As the two great champions closed in on the title, the tension was nearly unbearable. The majority of those in attendance rooted for Chrissie, their American sweetheart. But on this occasion it was Martina who would prevail, winning the final set and the title by the score of 4-6, 6-4, 6-4.

When John McEnroe and Jimmy Connors finally made their way on to the stadium court for Super Saturday's final contest, their starting time had been delayed for so long that they entered the arena like a couple of caged lions. In addition, the spine-tingling atmosphere was further charged by the electricity of night-time tennis at Flushing Meadows. Although the spectators had already sat through a long day, they sensed they were in for something special. And they were right. The three previous matches had set the bar at a daunting level but the charged up McEnroe and Connors jumped right over it. Playing some of the finest tennis of their respective careers, Mac and Jimmy slugged it out through four hard-fought sets.

And then it happened...with McEnroe leading five games to three in the fifth, he snatched the final point and thus edged out Connors by the score of 6-4, 4-6, 7-5, 4-6, 6-3. When the dust had finally settled it was 11:16 pm, and the lucky fans at courtside had witnessed 12 hours and 9 minutes of some of the most glorious tennis ever played. Now that's what I call getting your money's worth.

To be Young and In Paris

Michael Chang

Tennis's 18th most incredible moment occurred at the 1989 French Open. In 1989 the American Michael Chang had already become the youngest male player to win a main draw match when he won in the first round at the US Open at the age of 15 years, 6 months, and a month later became the first 'man' to reach a professional tournament semi-final when he did so at the Scottsdale event at the age of 15 years, 7 months. By the time the 1989 French Open came around the 17-year-old Chang had been consistently moving up the tennis ranks. Yet despite Chang's recent improvement he was considered no more than a long shot when Roland Garros began. What's more, the 19th-ranked Chang was fortunate to be seeded at all. When McEnroe and Muster were noticeably absent from the draw, Chang got lucky by moving into the 15th slot, the second-to-last seeded position. Additionally, there was the feeling around Paris and the tennis world that the Americans were jinxed at Roland Garros because an American male had not won the French Open in the 34 years since Tony Trabert was victorious on the red clay in 1955.

As the French Championships began, Chang worked his way through the first three rounds of the tournament without much difficulty. But in the fourth round it appeared to all that it was going to be a much different story for the 5′ 8″, 135-pound (61-kilo) Chinese-American. His opponent was none other than number one seeded, three-time champion Ivan Lendl. As the match got underway Chang seemed completely outclassed, as the powerful Czech took control by winning the first two sets, 6-4, 6-4. But as would be Chang's trademark for years to come, he came as if prepared for war. Even after winning the third set 6-3, however, the outlook seemed bleak for Chang when he started suffering from cramps in the fourth set. Predictably, the never-say-die little Rocky Balboa continued to fight both Lendl and the pain, and somehow won the set, 6-3.

As they fought into the fifth set Chang held a slight advantage when serving at 4-3, 15-30.

And then it happened...at this crucial point in the match Chang did the unthinkable. He served underhand. That's right, underhand! The flustered Lendl was caught completely off-guard and Chang won the point with the crowd roaring. Chang went on to win the game and take a 15-40 lead on Lendl's serve for double match point. At this juncture the newcomer Chang had one final trick up his sleeve. After Lendl's first serve missed, Chang moved way up to crowd the service line and bounced around excitedly, clearly an attempt to intimidate and unnerve the veteran Lendl. And to everyone's surprise, it worked! When the serve bounced off the net tape and went long, the victorious Chang fell to the court in utter exhaustion. And although a few critics thought Chang's 'shenanigans' were less than sporting, all agreed that they had witnessed one of the gutsiest, grittiest efforts ever seen in the history of the French Open.

But Chang wasn't finished, not by a long shot. After two long-fought, four-set wins in the quarters and semis, Chang found himself in his first Grand Slam final to face the third-seeded Swede, Stefan Edberg. With Edberg leading in the finals by two sets to one, Chang threw in one last Herculean effort to come back and win the match, and the championship, 6-2, 3-6, 4-6, 6-4, 6-2. In this tournament for the ages, the 17-year, 7-month-old Michael Chang became not only the youngest French Open Men's Champion in history, but also the youngest male ever to win any of the Grand Slam events. (Coincidentally, Arantxa Sanchez (later Sanchez-Vicario) matched Chang by also winning the women's title at age 17!)

The Streak

Roger Federer

Tennis's 17th most incredible moment spanned from Wimbledon 2005 through the 2007 US Open (ok, this is the last time I'll say it, 'Some moments last longer than others'). Question: What European country would be the most likely to have produced the world's top-ranked men's tennis player? If your answer was Switzerland, you must have been cheating. Top skier, maybe, or world-class mountain climber. But tennis? Nevertheless, on 8 August 1981, a newborn by the name of Roger Federer came into the world, and by the time he reached his teenage years he was already recognised for his world-class potential. As a youth, Roger also excelled at football, but with his tennis star rising he made the momentous choice that ultimately produced possibly the greatest player the sport has ever seen. (If this scenario sounds familiar, you're right...see incredible moment #74.)

Federer's career has been nothing short of phenomenal from day one. As a junior player his accolades included such awards as Junior Wimbledon champion, the prestigious Orange Bowl championship, and International Tennis Federation World Junior Champion of the year. Highly impressive, to say the least, but Roger's junior career pales in comparison to his professional accomplishments.

Credentials through the 2013 Wimbledon Championships:

- An incredible record 17 Grand Slam singles titles.
- The world's number one ranked player for a record 237 consecutive weeks from 2 February 2004 to 17 August 2008, and 302 weeks overall.
- Five consecutive Wimbledon titles from 2003–2007, which ties Bjorn Borg's modern era record (see incredible Moment #2).
- The sixth man (out of seven) to win all four grand slams in his career (see incredible Moment #7).
- 6 ATP World Tour Finals' Victories.
- The 2008 Olympic Doubles Gold Medal and the 2012 Olympic Singles Silver Medal.
- And for good measure, Roger holds the all-time career prize money record with over 75 million dollars.

But Federer's true greatness lies in his consistency. Tennis has seen many champions come and go. Yet rarely if ever have we had a male tennis player as consistently dominant. And when the sun has set on Roger's historic career, there is one statistic that will surely stand out above all the rest, namely 'The Streak'.

After losing in four sets in the semi-finals of the French Open to eventual champion Rafael Nadal, 'The Streak' began. Federer went on to defend his 2003 and 2004 Wimbledon titles by winning again in 2005. He would then reach the finals of the next nine consecutive Grand Slams, winning the titles at all of them except the 2006 and 2007 French Opens, where he lost the title matches again to his rival Rafael Nadal. In this era of extreme parity where any player can seemingly pull an upset on any given day, this record is nothing less than extraordinary!

As 2008 began, Roger was attempting to win his third consecutive Australian Open title. In typical Federer fashion, he ploughed through the draw to the semi-finals where he was matched up against third seeded Novak Djokovic. Although Roger held a lifetime 5-1 advantage and had beaten Novak in the US Open Finals a few months prior, Djokovic was not intimidated.

And then it happened...in an astonishing display of tennis mastery, Novak Djokovic dispatched the great Federer in straight sets 7-5, 6-3, 7-6 (7-5). Not only did this end Roger's amazing record of ten consecutive Grand Slam men's finals, but it was the first time he had lost in straight sets in any Grand Slam since the third round of the 2004 French Open. This match, and his 2008 loss to Rafael Nadal at Wimbledon (see incredible moment #1), has led to speculation that the young lions are about to push Federer aside. But it would be a mistake to conclude that this great player is no longer a force to be reckoned with. There are, in fact, two other noteworthy records. Federer also reached a record 23 consecutive grand slam semi-finals, and a record 36 consecutive grand slam quarter-finals. With a resume like Roger's, you can never count him out!

Burn Your Bras, You Can Afford It!

The Pioneers of Women's Tennis

Tennis's 16th most incredible moment occurred on 23 September 1970. Leading up to this episode was the growing success of the women's movement during the 1960s. As women began to assert themselves, it was no longer assumed that the image of an obedient mum in the kitchen should be the norm. And although women were making tremendous headway in many areas of our society, it appeared that women's sports were lagging behind. For example, Margaret Court had one of the most successful seasons a woman had ever seen in 1970 when she became only the third player, man or woman, to win a calendar Grand Slam (see incredible moment #47). Yet even with that historic season she earned approximately one quarter of Laver's winnings in a year that saw Laver fail to win a single Grand Slam event. Such discrimination is unthinkable by today's standards, but all of that was about to change.

A group of women tennis players, led by none other than the legendary Billie Jean King, decided that enough was enough. With the aid of the shrewd and determined businesswoman and activist, Gladys Heldman, they fought for change. The struggle really began when Heldman petitioned the Pacific Southwest Open chairman, Jack Kramer, to raise the women's prize money. When Kramer refused, a group of nine female players, lead by King, made the bold move to boycott the Los

Angeles event. Instead, the nine pioneers decided to play in a small tournament in Houston with a total measly purse of only $7,500 which was sponsored, in part, by Virginia Slims. In retaliation the United States Tennis Association said that they would not sanction the event, and even suspended the rebellious nine women from USTA events, including Grand Slam and Fed Cup competition. Undeterred, the women forged ahead.

And then it happened...each of the nine women signed symbolic one dollar contracts with Heldman to usher in a new era of women's tennis. And to the surprise of many, the tournament was an overwhelming success. Successful enough, in fact, that Virgina Slims decided to sponsor a full circuit of 19 tournaments the following year. As the newly founded Virgina Slims circuit became more and more successful, the USTA eventually lifted its ban. And by 1973, when Billie Jean King defeated Bobby Riggs in the famous 'Battle of the Sexes' (see incredible moment #3) the Women's tour had arrived. The USTA agreed to pair up with the Virginia Slims tour, and more importantly offer the men and women equal prize money at the US Open. Today, the players of the Women's Tennis Association are capable of making millions of dollars a year, and they owe it all to the courage of nine pioneering souls. I'm sure a thank you in the form of a large cheque would be appreciated. God knows today's players can afford it!

Prime Time

Ken Rosewall v. Rod Laver

Tennis's 15th most incredible moment occurred in 1972. Ken 'Muscles' Rosewall and Rod 'Rocket' Laver were two of the best players ever to compete on the court. The fellow Australians had outstanding careers by anyone's standards. Rosewall racked up 18 major titles in singles and doubles, while Laver amassed 20 of his own, becoming the only player to date to secure two calendar Grand Slams (see incredible moment #27). And although both players are now in the International Tennis Hall of Fame, the annals of tennis history do not do them justice due to their long absences from Grand Slam play before the Open Era of tennis. Yet despite their respective advanced ages in 1972, both men were still at the top of the game when they met in the WCT Tennis Finals in Dallas. As the match got underway at Moody Coliseum in front of 9,300 live spectators and a then record 22 million television spectators, Laver, the favourite, was trying to avenge his defeat to Rosewall in the 1971 WCT finals. And in case the viewing audience and the thrill of winning one of 1972's most prestigious tournaments wasn't motivation enough, the first-place prize money was a then-astounding $50,000. (In comparison, the 1972 Wimbledon Champions paycheque was a mere $10,000.) In addition, the winner would be presented with a diamond ring, a gold cup, and a brand new Lincoln Continental!

From the onset, the fans were treated to scintillating play. Laver jumped out to a five games to one lead and held on to take the first set, 6 -4. Rosewall fought back to take the second set at love and then jumped ahead by taking the third set, 6-3. Because of the outstanding level of play, NBC made the unprecedented decision to stick with the match and pre-empt its regularly scheduled programming. The situation looked grim for the Rocket as he went down 1-3 in the fourth set, but with a fighting spirit that characterised his career he fought back and took the set in a tiebreaker, 7-3. As the breathtaking shot making continued into the fifth set, the television audience was treated to a tennis match for the first time in prime time.

Rosewall jumped out to an early 4-1 lead. But once again Laver fought back to hold off a championship point at five games to four, and the two players fought to a tiebreaker which would decide the epic battle. With Laver holding a 5-4 advantage and two serves to come, it was now the exhausted 37-year-old Rosewall's turn to show his resolve. With two powerful returns of serve off his legendary backhand, Rosewall regained the lead, six points to five.

And then it happened...Rosewall gave it all he had with one final serve, and to his delight Laver's return landed harmlessly in the net. Game, set, championship, Rosewall, 4-6, 6-0, 6-3, 6-7, 7-6. Mike Davies, the director of the tournament, summed it up best when he said, 'Tennis was the real winner today. That was the greatest match I've ever seen.'

The King Goes to Court

Margaret Court v. Billie Jean King

Tennis's 14th most incredible moment occurred at the 1970 Wimbledon Championship Ladies final. Coming into the match, the 27-year-old Margaret Court had already won the Australian and French Open Championships earlier in the year, and she was half way to becoming only the second woman to win the Grand Slam. Furthermore, at this point in her career, Court was well on her way to becoming the most prolific Grand Slam winner in history (see incredible moment #47). On the other side of the 'Court' was Billie Jean King. King, who was 16 months younger than her archrival, was in the middle of making her own history. King's aggressive serve and volley style of play was perfectly suited for the fast grass courts of Wimbledon. And by the start of the 1970 Championships, she had already racked up an impressive three Wimbledon singles titles, five Wimbledon doubles titles and one Wimbledon mixed doubles title for a total of nine hoists of the coveted trophy to date. Yet as the two top women in the world stepped onto Centre Court for the finals, they did so gingerly because both were nursing injuries. Court had previously strained her ankle and King had a bad kneecap which would call for surgery right after the final. Nevertheless, both women knew that these opportunities were to be cherished and neither was ready to make excuses.

As the match got underway, the sell-out crowd sensed that they were in for a treat. The shot making was top-notch throughout the battle, and with the first set tied at six games apiece the women would have to fight on into extra games in this pre-tiebreaker era. Ultimately, the set would take on marathon proportions until Court was finally able to prevail, 14-12. Many women would have been devastated by such a strenuous setback, especially with an injury in tow, but King was a fighter throughout her career and today would be no different. Incredibly, the second set went much the same as the first until the competitors found themselves once again tied at six games all. At this point Court finally gained a 10-9 advantage. With the level of play at its zenith, especially when you consider the pressure of the moment, Court went for the kill.

And then it happened...Margaret Court captured the final game and the championship, 14-12, 11-9 in a two and a half hour slugfest which lasted a record 46 games, all of which were accumulated in a mere two sets of play. Court would eventually go on to win the Grand Slam in 1970 and King would ultimately amass a record 20 Wimbledon titles by 1979. But it was this epic battle in the 1970 Wimbledon finals that would go down in the annals of tennis history as one of the greatest matches ever played.

The Grand Don

Don Budge

Tennis's 13th most incredible moment occurred in 1938. John Donald Budge, known to all simply as Don, was born in Oakland, California on 13 June 1915. As a youth Don was a terrific athlete but fancied baseball, American football and basketball over tennis. Luckily for us, Budge eventually picked up a tennis racquet and found that he was able to wave it like a magic wand. As his skills improved, so did his interest in the game. In 1937 Don Budge became the number one amateur in the world. In that remarkable season he won Wimbledon and the US Championships, and led the United States to its first Davis Cup victory in 11 years. As 1937 came to an end Don had a big decision to make. Should he try to turn his fame into a lucrative pro career, or should he stick it out for one more year in the amateur ranks? Budge's decision finally came down to a debt of gratitude. Don was so indebted to what the great sport of tennis had done for him that he felt he owed it to the United States and to the game itself to play one more year as an amateur so he could help the US defend its Davis Cup crown.

This was a decision that would help make tennis history. It started at the Australian Championships. Budge, who was clearly the dominant player in the tournament, swept through the draw to win his first Grand Slam down under. Then, at the French, Budge had to deal with a bout of diarrhoea as well as a competitive field. Although he was forced to a fifth set by the Yugoslavian, Franjo Kukuljevic, he eventually reached the final where he easily defeated Roderich Menzel of Czechoslovakia in straight sets. It was then on to Wimbledon where the 6' 1'' redhead swept through the tournament without losing a set. And to top it off, Budge pulled off the rare triple by winning the doubles and mixed doubles titles as well. Finally, in the US Championships, the year's last Grand Slam, Budge had made his way to the finals where he was to play his friend, Gene Mako, his doubles partner and Davis Cup teammate.

And then it happened...in front of 12,000 fans John Donald Budge defeated Mako by the score of 6-3, 6-8, 6-2, 6-1 to become the first man or woman to win tennis's Grand Slam! Incredibly, at each of the four Slam events, Budge suffered from an illness or injury. And apparently to put the icing on the cake on what many consider to be one of the finest years a tennis player has ever had, Budge successfully lead the US to its second straight Davis Cup title. Don Budge, who was inducted into the International Tennis Hall of Fame in 1964 and passed away on 26 January 2000, will always be remembered as the first man or woman to pull off tennis's most impressive feat...the Grand Slam!

Hitler the Tennis Fan?

Don Budge v. Gottfried Von Cramm

Tennis's 12th most incredible moment occurred in 1937. It involved the freckle-faced, redheaded American Don Budge, and the blond-haired, green-eyed German Baron Gottfried Von Cramm, in a Davis Cup Interzone final with the winner to play England for the cup title. A couple of weeks earlier the number one seeded Budge easily defeated the second-seeded Von Cramm in the Wimbledon final, 6-3, 6-4, 6-2. This time the two men would meet again on the same court, the most famous court in all of tennis – Centre Court at Wimbledon – to determine which country would advance to the Davis Cup finals. With the countries tied at two matches apiece it all came down to the final match between the respective teams' two best players, Budge and Von Cramm. The contestants were in the locker room preparing for battle with a packed stadium, headlined by the queen herself waiting in eager anticipation.

And then it happened...with the threat of World War II looming and the Davis Cup at stake, the telephone rang. The caller? None other than the Fuhrer himself, Adolf Hitler, who was reportedly infuriated that a non-Aryan by the name of Jessie Owens had dominated the Olympics the year before. Hitler had called to let Von Cramm know how important it was that he win for the fatherland. Von Cramm, a noted anti-Nazi, entered the court pale and shaken. Yet despite the added pressure, or maybe due to it, the underdog Von Cramm came out on fire playing the best tennis of his life. In fact, Von Cramm jumped out to an 8-6, 7-5 lead. But the 22-year-old American would not be deterred and fought back gallantly to win the next two sets, 6-4, 6-2, and even the match. With the tennis being played at the highest of levels, Von Cramm once again took control to lead the fifth and final set, 4 games to 1. With a desperate situation in front of him, Budge made the very risky tactical decision to attack Von Cramm's serve. The decision worked. Budge was able to get the break back and even the set at 4 games all.

As the match progressed and the tension increased, so did the level of play. Finally, Budge was able to break Von Cramm's serve again and take a 7-6 lead, thus gaining the chance to serve for the match. But this time it was Von Cramm's chance to show his resolve. One, two, three, four times Budge held match points, and four times Von Cramm fought them off. On the fifth match point there was a long rally. Von Cramm took control of the point by hitting a hard crosscourt forehand and following it to the net. As Budge streaked to the ball he took a wild swing and fell to the ground. The result of this extraordinary effort was a perfectly placed passing shot that landed six inches inside both lines. Game, Set, Match, USA.

Budge later stated, 'It was the greatest shot I ever made'. As the two combatants came to the net in near darkness, Von Cramm said, 'This was absolutely the finest match I have ever played in my life. I'm very happy that I could have played it against you, whom I like so much. Congratulations.' The two men, who were actually good friends, then hugged each other in an act of mutual admiration. A week later the US would then go on to defeat England in the finals, 4-1, to take the Davis Cup title back to the States for the first time in 11 years. Upon their return to New York, the American tennis heroes were greeted by a well-deserved ticker-tape parade.

Comeback Cochet

Henry Cochet

Tennis's 11th most incredible moment occurred at the 1927 Wimbledon Championships. This story relates to the diminutive, 145-pound (65-kilo) battling Frenchman, Henri Cochet. During Cochet's Hall of Fame career, he amassed four French Championship titles, two Wimbledons, and one US crown. Yet it was during the 1927 Wimbledon tournament where the fourth-seeded Cochet put on a performance that would be remembered for generations to come. Cochet had made his way through the draw and found himself in a quarter-final match-up with Frank Hunter.

And then it happened...Cochet was down two sets to love to Hunter before he was able to turn the match around and emerge victorious, 3-6, 3-6, 6-2, 6-2, 6-4. Now you may be saying to yourself, 'impressive, but is that really worthy of the 11th most incredible moment in tennis history?' Well, keep reading, because in the next round Cochet's opponent was none other than Hunter's doubles partner, the legendary Big Bill Tilden, and once again Cochet found himself down two sets to love. But this time he was down 5-1 in the third set, and with all due respect to Hunter, he was no Bill Tilden.

And then it happened again...With the score 5-1, 15 all, Cochet unbelievably turned the match completely around by winning the next 17 points in a row! In one of the greatest comebacks against a legendary player that tennis has ever seen, Cochet ended up winning the match 3-6, 4-6, 7-5, 6-4, 6-3. This accomplishment, in itself, was certainly noteworthy, but Cochet still had one more match between himself and his first Wimbledon title. Cochet's opponent in the final was fellow Frenchman Jean Borotra, and you guessed it, Cochet was once again down two sets to love.

And then it happened for the third and final time!...First, Cochet somehow managed to even the match at two sets apiece. But in the fifth set he had to dig himself out of yet another deep hole. With the score five games to two against him, he held off a match point to make the score 5-3. Then, with Borotra serving for the championship, Cochet staved off an incredible five more championship points and eventually came back to win the title, 4-6, 4-6, 6-3, 6-4, 7-5. Not only had Cochet come back in three successive rounds from two sets to love down, but all three men he defeated – Hunter, Tilden and Borotra – would end up in the International Hall of Fame. It would not be long before the odds evened out, however. As the expression goes, 'what goes around comes around', and in the doubles final Cochet and his partner, Jacques Brugnon, led none other than the team of Hunter and Tilden by, you guessed it, two sets to love before losing the match, 1-6, 4-6, 8-6, 6-3, 6-4. Now that's what I call tennis karma!

Class on Grass

Roger Federer v. Rafael Nadal

Tennis's 10th most incredible Moment occurred in the 2007 Wimbledon Gentlemen's Final. Tennis pundits often debate the question of history's premier male player. The list is filled with iconic names: Tilden, LaCoste, Laver, Connors, McEnroe, to name a few. But when tennis supremacy is defined, sooner or later the discussion turns to Wimbledon and who deserves to lay claim to the title King of the All England Club.

Bjorn Borg has long been considered one of the greatest Wimbledon champions of all time, and he has the hardware to prove it. The stoic Swede, who was often characterised as having ice water in his veins, defied the conventional wisdom which stated one could only win by coming to net on the lightning fast Wimbledon grass. Instead Bjorn was also able to succeed from the baseline, often stroking laser passing shots from both wings. Using this counterpunching strategy, Borg set a modern-day record five straight Wimbledon titles from 1976–1980. And to top it off, his 1980 finals victory over rival John McEnroe is universally considered a match for the ages (see incredible moment #2). Until the arrival of Pete Sampras, Borg's record was thought to be unassailable.

Unlike Borg, Pete played a very aggressive serve and volley game, and in view of his dominance on grass it appeared that he might lay claim to the Wimbledon trophy until he retired. But in 2001 along came Roger

Federer. Roger also used serve and volley tactics at times, but in a decidedly different manner. Where Pete stalked the court, banging in huge serves and cracking winner first volleys, Roger's style could be described as silky smooth. Big serve and crisp volleys to be sure, but combined with elegant but penetrating ground strokes that were beautiful to behold. Sampras met Federer in the fourth round and that would prove to be Pete's undoing. Roger won the match, ending Sampras' attempt at five in a row and an eighth overall Wimbledon title.

At that point it looked like Borg's record of five straight championships would likely stand the test of time, but Federer's victory over the great Sampras was a harbinger of things to come. After a disappointing early round loss in 2002, Roger apparently decided that he really didn't enjoy losing on grass, and a year later he won his first Wimbledon title by defeating Mark Philippoussis in the Centre Court finale. That was followed by wins over Andy Roddick in both the 2004 and 2005 finals, and then came title number four in 2006, as he went on to defeat his arch rival, the superbly talented Rafael Nadal.

With four in a row, Federer now had history in his grasp. However, after a devastating 2007 French Open defeat at the hands of his nemesis, Nadal, Roger was too exhausted to compete in the Gerry Weber Open in Halle, the Wimbledon grass court warm-up event that he had won before each of his previous Wimbledon victories. Yet true to form, he breezed through the tournament and once again met Nadal for the title.

While a Wimbledon final is always a stunning spectacle, this time it held an extra degree of importance because Federer had a chance to make history by tying the record of five straight championships. Even Bjorn Borg, who had rarely attended a tennis match since his abrupt retirement from the sport in 1981, was at Centre Court to witness the dramatic event.

The match started off well for Federer as he won the first set in a tiebreaker, nine points to seven. But Nadal, the consummate fighter, dug in to take the second set, 6-4, evening the match. When Federer won the tightly contested third set, once again in a tiebreaker, tennis glory was within reach. But for a second time Nadal turned the tables, decisively taking set number four at 6-2, and pushing Roger to his first Wimbledon fifth set since his 2001 victory over Sampras. And what a fifth set it would be! At 1-1 and 2-2, Federer faced pivotal break points at 15-40 but was able to recover, holding serve in both cases. Roger then rode an emotional high to break Nadal, and after holding serve to go up 5-2, the Swiss Magician was in position to pull off what was once thought to be unachievable.

And then it happened...on his second match point, Federer attacked the net and knocked off one last volley winner to secure his place in Wimbledon history. As Roger fell to his knees, the appreciative Wimbledon crowd, led by Bjorn Borg himself, gave both players a well-deserved standing ovation. After the match, the classy Roger Federer spoke to BBC sport as he fought back tears. *'Each one is special but to play a champion like Rafa, it means a lot, and equalling Bjorn's record as well....He (Nadal) is a fantastic player and he's going to be around so much longer, so I'm happy with every one I get before he takes them all.'*

As always, Roger was gracious in victory, but his reference to Nadal would prove to be prophetic, as the tenacious Rafael would return the following year to exact his revenge (see incredible moment #1).

Forever Young

Jimmy Connors

Tennis's 9th most incredible moment occurred at the 1991 US Open. When one speaks of memorable US Open moments, there's always a good chance that Jimmy Connors will be involved. This moment would be no different. Connors holds the Open Era record for men with five US Open singles titles (tied with Sampras and Federer) and is the only man to have won the tournament on three different surfaces (see incredible moment #52). Despite all of Connors' great accomplishments at the US Open and as a player in general, many consider his shining moment to be his run at the US Open in 1991. But few could have predicted Connors' spectacular display before the tournament got underway. In 1990, due to a wrist injury, Connors only played in three matches and lost all three. Consequently, by the end of the year his ranking was an abysmal 936th in the world. And although Connors was able to work his ranking back to a somewhat more respectable number 174 at the beginning of the 1991 US Open, he still needed a wild-card entry just to qualify for the tournament.

When Connors was playing his first-round match against John McEnroe's younger brother, Patrick, it looked like it was going to be an early exit for the 'old man Connors' who would turn an ancient (in tennis terms) 39 years of age during the tournament. Connors was down two sets to love and 3-0 in the third set before the magic began. As everyone in the stadium was writing him off, Jimmy wouldn't stop battling. And unbelievably, 4 hours and 18 minutes after the match began, Connors had emerged victorious, 4-6, 6-7, 6-4, 6-2, 6-4, at 1:35 am!

But Jimbo was just getting started. Gaining the momentum, Connors dismissed Michiel Schapers and tenth-seeded Karel Novacek, both in straight sets in the second and third rounds, respectively. These victories set up a 2 September 39th birthday celebration with fellow American and friend, Aaron Krickstein. Krickstein led the fourth-round encounter by two sets to one, but Connors, as usual, continued to fight. And although Jimmy was able to secure the fourth set 6-3, Krickstein, who had one of the best five set records in tennis, jumped out to a 5-2 fifth set lead. Twice in the final set Connors was two points away from defeat but was somehow able to extend the match to a tiebreaker. And with the crowd in a frenzy, Connors didn't disappoint. Jimmy won the tiebreaker and the match as the delighted crowd sang happy birthday to the aging veteran.

Although eight men had now advanced to the quarter-final round, all eyes were on Connors. In Jimmy's next match, a night-time event against Paul Haarhuis, touts were receiving as much as $500 per ticket. Yet as it turned out the scalpers were the ones who got taken. With Connors down 6-4, 5-4, Haarhuis was serving for a commanding two-sets-to-love lead. But Connors and his never-say-die attitude worked his way to an all-important break point.

And then it happened... In a point that is considered to be one of the best ever played at the US Open, Haarhuis worked his way to the net, leaving Connors with no recourse but to throw up a defensive lob. As Haarhuis hit the overhead, Connors was able to track it down and throw up another lob. This was followed by another overhead and yet another lob. Before the point would end, Haarhuis had hit four, yes four, seemingly point-ending overheads, but the scrappy Connors had returned them all. Now, with the crowd literally jumping out of their seats, Jimmy ended the point with a spectacular running backhand passing shot down the line to obtain the crucial break of serve. As Connors pumped his arms in the air the crowd erupted in jubilation. At this point Haarhuis might as well have packed up his bags and headed for home, because he was now playing against 20,000 screaming New Yorkers as well as his formidable opponent. Almost mercifully, Jimmy finally dusted the Dutchman, 4-6, 7-6, 6-4, 6-2. The ageless wonder had become the first wildcard to advance to the US Open semi-finals.

Jimmy's magical run would abruptly come to an end with a straight-set defeat at the hands of Jim Courier, who in turn would eventually lose the final to Stephan Edberg. Yet this US Open would always be remembered as the one in which the irrepressible, ageless Jimmy Connors gave the New York crowd a look into the past, and a thrill they would remember long into the future.

Sometimes the Best Opponent Is a Bad One

Arthur Ashe v. Jimmy Connors

Tennis's 8th most incredible moment occurred at the 1975 Wimbledon final. The combatants for the event were the 22-year-old American Jimmy Connors versus his 31-year-old fellow countryman, Arthur Ashe. The fiery Connors was coming off what would be his best year on tour in which he won three Grand Slam titles and 99 of 103 matches. Furthermore, Connors appeared to be at the top of his game when, as the defending champion, he rolled into the 1975 finals without losing a set. On the other hand, the six-seeded Ashe seemed destined to be a bridesmaid once again. Although Ashe had won the US Open in 1968 and followed that up with an Australian Open championship in 1970, he had been major-less ever since. Furthermore, the analytical Ashe seemed to think himself right out of his big matches, which was evidenced by the fact that he had lost 14 of his previous 19 finals. On the day of the championship match, the confident Connors was made a heavy 10 to 1 favourite by local bookmakers. And just to add a little spice to the mix, two weeks before the final, Connors had filed a five million dollar libel law suit against Ashe, the Association of Tennis Professionals president, for having called Jimmy 'unpatriotic' for his decision not to participate in Davis Cup play for the good old US of A. Ashe responded by walking onto Centre Court for the finals wearing his blue Davis Cup warm-up suit with the red letters 'USA' proudly displayed on the chest.

As the match began, it was evident that the over-analysing,

underdog Ashe had come up with a game plan that appeared brilliant. Arthur had put together a strategy to throw off the counter-punching heavy favourite. It was well documented that Connors loved to feed off a big hitter's power game. Consequently, Ashe decided to give Jimmy a bunch a junk shots that would induce errors from the normally consistent Connors. As Ashe sliced slow forehands and backhands and hit three-quarter speed serves out wide, the unthinkable began to happen. Connors began to make one unforced error after another, allowing Ashe to jump out to a 6-1, 6-1 lead. And when Ashe was up 3-2 with a break in the third set it looked like he might pull off a feat that the bookmakers had listed at 40-1; beat Connors in straight sets. The bookies breathed a temporary sigh of relief as Connors's competitive spirit didn't die and he fought back to take the third set, 7-5. Yet even when Connors took a three games to love lead in the fourth set, Ashe would not abandon his strategy. And sure enough, Arthur regained the lead. Finally, at match point Ashe hit yet another slice serve out wide to Connors' backhand. Jimmy's defensive return was a sitting duck for Ashe's volley winner.

And then it happened...Ashe put away the easy volley and in doing so made history by becoming the first male African-American Wimbledon champion!

The Fine Line to Immortality

Roger Federer

Tennis's 7th most incredible moment occurred at the 2009 French Open. As the major championship in Paris got underway there was more than the Musketeers' cup on the line. For one, Rafael Nadal was vying to become the first man or woman to win five straight French Open titles, and he was the prohibitive favorite to repeat as the champion on the terre batu. Rafa was not only the current world's number one but was also dominating the game. Nadal had already won the year's first grand slam in Australia and to make things even more ominous for his competitors he had never lost a match in his career as the king of clay at Roland Garros. And incredibly, Nadal had never even been pushed to a fifth set.

On the opposite side of the draw the current world's number two was also desperate to claim his spot in history. Not only was Roger Federer only one grand slam shy of the great Pete Sampras' record of fourteen but if he could add this milestone to his immense resume he would also become only the sixth man in history to win all four grand slams in his career. Despite the fact that Federer had just won the clay court tune up in Madrid defeating Nadal in a straight set final, most tennis pundits were not giving Roger a snowball's chance in hell to overcome his Achilles heal. For one, as previously mentioned, Rafa was considered unbeatable at the French and came into the tournament in prime form. And secondly, many so called experts stated that if the unthinkable were to occur, and Nadal did not repeat as champion, then it would surely be Djokovic, or Murray, or even a dark horse like the Frenchman Monfils who would claim the title. Roger Federer was an after thought. But as history has taught us, never count out a great champion.

As the tournament got underway there was little to dissuade the notion that the Majorcan front runner would not disappoint. After cruising through the first two rounds in straight sets he pummeled the former world number one, Leyton Hewitt, 6-1, 6-3, 6-1 in the third round and appeared to be in his typical stellar form. On the other hand, 'FedEx' was not having such an easy go at it. After winning his first round is straight sets he had to use all of his grand slam guile to pull out a second round encounter with the little known Jose Acasuso coming back from a set apiece and 1-5 in the third to win in four. And in the third round had to fight back yet again after losing the first set to Mathieu to once again win in four. In fact, at this point many were speculating that this may, in fact, be the tournament where Roger's record streak of nineteen straight appearances in grand slam semifinals came to an end.

And then it happened...in one of the greatest upsets in grand slam history the talented but unheralded Swede, Robin Soderling, who had never been past the third round in any grand slam tournament previous to this year's French, played the match of his life and shocked the tennis world by overpowering Nadal and sending him packing in four sets.

The buzz around the grounds was immediate and all of the sudden the tournament was wide open. Many of the top players realized that they now had a legitimate chance at this title that just hours earlier appeared to be a forgone conclusion. But with opportunity comes pressure and now the weight of the tennis world was on Federer. Roger, who had lost to Nadal four straight years at the French, the last three coming in the finals, knew that he would never have a better chance at immortality than he would right now. And in the very next round his play seemed to exemplify the added pressure as he dropped the first two sets to the German Tommy Haas. But in true Federer greatness he once again called on his champion resolve to come back and win in five. And when Federer defeated the dangerous Monfils in straight sets in the quarterfinals he was now the prohibitive favorite to take the title and make history. As the top players continued to fall throughout the two-week bloodbath, Roger was now set to face the Argentine, Juan Martin Del

Potro, in the semifinals. And in case Federer needed a little comfort to calm his nerves he could look to his previous five encounters with Del Potro in which he never dropped a set. But this day would be different as the tall, lanky South American played with reckless abandon and inconceivably took a two sets to one advantage. But as driven by destiny the great Roger Federer found a way to pull victory from the jaws of defeat yet again to win in five.

On the top half of the draw Soderling avoided the presumed let down after his monumental upset of Nadal and carried his momentum all the way to the finals. Once again, if Roger needed to still his raw emotions he could look to history as he had not lost a match in his nine previous encounters with the dangerous Swede. But this was not the same Robin Soderling and this was no typical day at the office. As the finals got underway the pro-Federer Parisian crown was not disappointed as Roger cruised in the first set six games to one. But with Federer up two games to one in the second the unexpected happened as a spectator ran out onto the court and actually made contact with Roger before being tackled by security and dragged off the court. As play continued questions immediately came to mind. Would the incident rattle the normally unflappable champion? Could this be the impetus for a Soderling comeback? And when Federer lost the following game at love the tension in the stadium was palpable. But once again Fed was able to call on his vast experience and compose himself eventually taking the set in a tiebreak, which he would later call "one of the greatest tiebreakers in my career," seven points to one. With history in the making, even the light rain falling couldn't diminish the moment. With Federer serving at five games to four he finally held championship point as the electric stadium crowd and millions more around the globe held their collective breath.

And then it happened again...Federer struck one last mighty serve, and as the Soderling return landed meekly in the net, Roger the champion fell to his knees in triumph. As the incomparable Swiss Magician held the revered trophy, tears streamed down his face. By many accounts Roger could now be considered the greatest player to have ever played the game. But in order to leave no doubt Roger Federer would need one more major victory...(see incredible moment #6).

The Greatest of All Time

Roger Federer v. Andy Roddick

Tennis's 6th most incredible moment occurred at the 2009 Gentlemen's Wimbledon Final. As long as the great sport of tennis has been played there has been one question that has perplexed all that love the game: Who is the greatest of all time? Yet the answer isn't as straight forward as it may initially appear. What criteria should be enlisted in determining greatness? Should it be the number of weeks ranked at number one? Success on multiple surfaces? Grace under pressure? There are so many factors to consider that it can make one's head spin. While the debate is sure to continue, almost all will concede that winning grand slam tournaments is at the top of the list. As in any sport, at the end of the day holding the champion's trophy is what matters most and tennis is no different.

After Roger Federer captured the 2009 French Open (see incredible moment #7) and tied Pete Sampras' grand slam singles title record at fourteen, he certainly had the pedigree to be considered the greatest ever. Yet there were still several doubters that would not proclaim the great Swiss master as the best to ever pick up a racquet until he held this most prestigious of records for himself. Consequently, coming into the 2009 Wimbledon Championships Roger knew that he was at history's doorstep. And even though Federer had won this most elite of titles five times previously, and his main nemesis Rafael Nadal had to withdraw prior to the tournament due to injury, all knowledgeable students of the game, especially Roger himself, knew that a fifteenth major championship was far from a forgone conclusion.

Despite the pressure of rewriting the record books, 'Fed Ex' seemed to be a player possessed. Match after match Roger seemed to elevate his level of play, and going into the championship final he had conceded only one set. However, the man standing between Federer and history was the dangerous American Andy Roddick. While it was true that Roger held an 18-2 lifetime record over Roddick, Andy was in the midst of what some were calling a career resurrection. After several years without the opportunity to compete in a grand slam final, A-Rod was playing some of the most inspired tennis of his career. After a gutsy five set quarterfinal victory over the 2002 Wimbledon Champion Leyton Hewitt, Roddick shocked the tennis world and disappointed the hometown Wimbledon crowd by taking out the Scot, Andy Murray, in what many were calling one of the greatest matches of Roddick's career. And with a serve that was considered one of the best weapons in the game, and a huge forehand to go along with it, Andy surely had a 'puncher's chance' of taking the title and upsetting the thousands of fans who came to witness history in the making.

As the finals got underway, Centre Court was playing faster than normal due to the surprisingly dry conditions throughout the fortnight. While the speed of a grass court has always favored a big serve, the effects of the dry spell were now magnified with two of the best servers in the game battling for the title. With each man easily holding serve, one could sense that the title would come down to converting on the critical break points. As the first set came to a close, Federer had four break opportunities at five games apiece but Roddick held firm. Then, in the very next game, Andy converted his only break point of the first set to win seven games to five. And as the second set progressed it became clear that Roddick was cracking his booming serves with pinpoint accuracy. As the set went to a tiebreak, Roddick, who had one of the best tiebreak records of 2009 to date, held a commanding six points to two advantage. If he could convert on just one of the next four points he would have a stranglehold on the match.

And then it happened...Federer, with his back against the wall, played inspired tennis and the seemingly unflappable Roddick appeared to feel the pressure of the moment as Roger reeled off six straight points to take the set and even the finals at one set apiece. Both men continued to hold serve throughout the third set, leading to another tiebreaker. Once again Federer prevailed, this time by a score of seven points to five. Federer now had the lead and the momentum. And to make things more ominous for the American, Roger was known to be at his best when he had a lead. But to Roddick's credit he kept his composure and shocked the All-England crowd by breaking Federer to win the fourth set, six games to three.

It was now two sets each. If Federer was to make history he would need to accomplish what he had yet to do thus far...break Roddick's thunderous serve. But this would continue to prove to be no easy task. Luckily for Roger his serve was also holding up marvelously. Yet with no final set tiebreaker at Wimbledon, it would take a break of serve to hold tennis' most coveted title. With the fifth set now into extra games the tension was riveting. Finally, at eight games all, Roddick held two break points when Federer served at 15-40. However, this time Roger showed off his champion's resolve by staving off both pivotal points, and went on to hold. The two gladiators battled on and on. With Andy serving at fifteen games to sixteen, Federer finally held his first break point of the longest fifth set in the history of the Wimbledon championship final.

And then it happened again...the gallant Roddick finally miss-hit a forehand long and it was over! With some of the most accomplished champions in the history of the sport looking on from the royal box, led by none other than Pistol Pete Sampras himself, Roger Federer had made history. Just by stepping onto the court, Roger was playing in his record-breaking twentieth men's grand slam singles final as well as his record seventh consecutive Wimbledon final. In securing his sixth Wimbledon title, Roger had also won the longest All-England final in terms of games played with seventy-seven, the longest fifth set in grand slam final's history with thirty, and had become only the second man since 1980 to sweep the French Open and Wimbledon in the same year equaling the feat of his chief rival, Rafael Nadal, from the previous year (see incredible

Who Said Love Means Nothing In Tennis

Suzanne Lenglen v. Helen Wills

Tennis's 5th most incredible moment occurred on 16 February 1926. This moment involved a match between the two best women who had ever played the game until that point in history. In that year the 26-year-old flamboyant Frenchwoman Suzanne Lenglen was at the pinnacle of her career. She had already racked up six Wimbledon titles and had only lost one match in a seven-year stretch...and that was a default due to illness! (See incredible moment #59.) Her opponent that day was Helen Wills, an American university student. Although Wills would eventually capture many Grand Slam titles in an illustrious career, in 1926 her talents were still beginning to blossom. Early in the year, Wills began playing tournaments in the South of France in an obvious attempt to set up a showdown with Lenglen. When La Grande Suzanne heard of Helen 'Little Miss Poker Face' Wills' plan, Lenglen stated, 'This girl must be mad. Does she think she can come and beat me on my home court?' The anticipation for what was being called 'the battle of the century' reached a fever pitch.

At an insignificant tournament in Cannes, France, the two legendary players would finally meet for their one and only encounter. With hundreds of reporters and photographers present, the crowd of 3,000, including kings, barons and distinguished guests from around the world, packed the stadium and paid a then unheard-of $12 per ticket. Others stood on top of roofs and cars, climbed ladders and trees, or did whatever they could to catch a glimpse of history in the making. As the match got underway, excitement filled the air. And even though Lenglen's parents had harangued her about winning until 2:30 that morning, she came out playing flawless tennis. In fact, it was Wills who appeared to be nervous as Lenglen secured the first set, six games to three. But Wills, who was showing the skills and determination that would make her one of the all time greats, fought back to take a 3-1 lead in the second set. Just when it looked like the tide was turning, Lenglen stepped it up a notch and regained the lead. With a 6-5, 40-15 Lenglen advantage, Wills hit a forehand into the corner that was called out. Game, set and match, Lenglen.

And then it happened... As the two women were fighting off the crowd to shake hands at the net, the linesman, Lord Charles Hope, advised the renowned Wimbledon umpire George Hillyard that in fact the ball had been good and that a fan had made the call of out. After order was restored Wills fought back to win the game and even the set at six games apiece. But Lenglen did not have to wait long for her third match point. She quickly regained her composure, and two games later, after 63 minutes of play, she finally finished off her opponent with an overhead smash. Lenglen had defeated Wills by a score of 6-3, 8-6 in front of the cheering, partisan French crowd. After the match the previously haughty Lenglen sat down and began to sob tears of joy and relief.

And what, may you ask, became of Helen Wills? As she was preparing to leave the court a young man jumped over the fence, approached her, and in an attempt to console her, said, 'Miss Wills, you played awfully well.' That young man's name was Fred Moody, and four years later Helen Wills would become Helen Wills Moody. *Miss* Wills may have lost the match, but it's a safe bet that *Mrs.* Wills wouldn't have swapped her consolation prize for the victory.

Terror on the Court

Monica Seles v. Gunther Parche

Tennis's 4th most incredible moment occurred on 30 April 1993. The world's number one player, Monica Seles, had been dominating the women's tennis circuit for over two years. Since bursting onto the tour as a teenager, Seles had already accumulated eight Grand Slam titles and had the momentum of a locomotive, wining seven of the previous nine. Seles had clearly replaced her chief rival, Steffi Graf, as the world's best player. Now, at 19 years of age, Seles was potentially on pace to compile the greatest record in tennis history.

And then it happened...Seles was engaged in a quarter-final match against Bulgarian Magdalena Maleeva at the Citizen Cup tournament in Hamburg, Germany. With Seles leading in the second set, the competitors were sitting on either side of the umpire's chair on the changeover when Gunther Parche, a 38-year-old unemployed lathe operator, reached over a barricade and stabbed Seles with a 9-inch boning knife between her shoulder blades. Seles let out a terrifying shriek before collapsing on the court. While Seles' physical wounds were not as serious as they could have been (doctors said the knife narrowly missed the spinal cord, which could have resulted in death), the psychological effects of the attack were devastating. Subsequently, Seles was off the tour for 27 months.

The obvious question is why any person could commit such a heinous act. The rationale...so that the deranged Parche could see his favourite player, Steffi Graf, return to the number one ranking. And ironically, that's exactly what happened. Graf reclaimed the top spot during Seles' absence and went on to dominate women's tennis before retiring to private life. Although Seles returned to professional tennis in 1995, and was a perennial top ten player after the attack, she was never the unstoppable force of her earlier years. While Seles had won eight Grand Slam tournaments prior to the stabbing, since then she won only one more, the 1996 Australian Open. And although Parche was found guilty of grievous bodily harm in October of 1993, he was only given a suspended sentence due to the fact that the trial judge, Elke Bosse, ruled that Parche was emotionally unbalanced and may not have been completely responsible for his actions. Consequently, Parche has never spent a day in jail. In protest of the sentence, Seles never again played a tournament in Germany since that infamous day in 1993.

Battle of the Sexes

Billie Jean King v. Bobby Riggs

Tennis's 3rd most incredible moment occurred on 20 September 1973. This story began several months earlier when Bobby Riggs, the 55-year-old former Wimbledon champion and self-proclaimed 'King of the Male Chauvinist Pigs', played Margaret Smith Court who at the time was the number one woman's player in the world. Although Court won a total of 18 tournaments, and three of the four Grand Slam events in 1973, Riggs boisterously stated to whomever would listen that women were inferior athletes to men and therefore even a man well past his prime with 'one foot in the grave' could defeat a woman at the top of her sport. Eventually Court took the bait, and Riggs, the ultimate hustler and showman, intimidated and unnerved her so badly that he easily won the match by the humiliating score of 6-2, 6-1. Because this spectacle took place on Mother's Day it soon became known as the Mother's Day Massacre. But this wasn't the end of the story. In fact this match became the precursor to what many sports historians call one of the most important moments in women's sports history.

In the aftermath of his one-sided victory Riggs's gloating became even more insufferable, but a response soon came in the person of Billy Jean King, Margaret Court's top-ranked counterpart. Riggs was challenged to a re-match, this time against Billy Jean who was determined to exact revenge on behalf of women everywhere. After some initial give-and-take taunting, Riggs and King agreed to what would come to be known around the world as 'The Battle of the Sexes'. The hype for this event quickly reached epic proportions. It was like no other tennis match ever played, and the media attention catalysed Riggs into a frenzy of showmanship. No stranger to a camera or microphone, Riggs grabbed the spotlight at every opportunity and consistently tried to play mind games with King in an attempt to unnerve her as he had successfully done with Court. But Billie Jean held firm. King was quoted as saying, 'I realised the one thing Bobby wanted me to do was get caught up in everything. He's a hustler, but in order to hustle you, he's got to see you, know where you are, keep tabs on you. I felt if I hid from him, if I wasn't around physically, it would drive him nuts.'

And then it happened...The historic day of 20 September 1973 finally came. In a rock concert atmosphere there were 30,472 fans waiting to watch 'The Battle Of The Sexes' in the Houston Astrodome, the largest crowd ever to watch a tennis match live. In addition, approximately 48 million more from 37 countries were glued to their television sets.

King entered the stadium first, carried in on a golden throne by five men wearing togas. Riggs followed in a rickshaw being pulled by six 'well-endowed' women, aptly named 'Bobby's Bosom Buddies'. Early in the match Riggs must have realised that King was not going to be as easy a foe as her predecessor. With Riggs serving at 1-2 and 15 all in the first set, the adversaries played a gruelling point with King retrieving shot after shot. And although Riggs won that point when King eventually hit a backhand wide, Riggs was clearly winded. In celebration, he could only bend over at the waist and smile at the floor. As the match continued, Riggs, who had previously stated, 'I have no nerves', clearly got a case of the jitters when, while serving at 4-5, 30-40, he double faulted to lose the first set. King then carried her momentum through the second set, winning it 6-3, and finally into the third, winning again 6-3 to take the match in 2 hours and 4 minutes, thus earning the winner-take-all prize money of 100,000 dollars.

Kings and Riggs both accomplished legendary feats in their respective Hall of Fame careers. In 1939 Riggs won the Wimbledon triple, sweeping the singles, doubles and mixed doubles championships all in the same year (see incredible moment #26). King was the first woman in any sport to amass over 100,000 dollars (sixty thousand pounds) in prize money in a single year ($117,000 in 1971) and she captured 39 Grand Slam titles between 1961 and 1980. Yet Riggs and King will be remembered first and foremost for participating in one of the most significant events in twentieth-century sports. And Mrs. King, in her own right, will be remembered for winning the match that helped open doors for women's athletics all over the world.

A Match for the Ages

Bjorn Borg v. John McEnroe

Tennis's 2nd most incredible moment occurred in the Wimbledon final on 5 July 1980. This match is considered by sports historians, luminaries, fans and just about everyone with a heartbeat, to be one of the greatest tennis match ever played, as well as one of the best sporting events of the twentieth century. It featured the 24-year-old Swedish heartthrob Bjorn Borg versus the brash 21-year-old American John McEnroe. One of the many things that made this match so memorable was the incredible contrast between the participants, not only in playing styles but in their temperaments as well. Borg, the right-handed baseliner, was the world's established number one player whereas the left-handed McEnroe was an attacking serve-and-volleyer, desperate for Borg's elite title as the world's best. The stoic Borg played as if he had ice water in his veins, while the volatile McEnroe played with a fire in his belly. And the only thing the English crowd and press seemed to enjoy doing more than praising Borg for his superb level of play and sportsmanlike conduct was to lambaste McEnroe for his tantrums and immature behaviour. Added to this mix was the fact that Borg was vying for his fifth straight Wimbledon crown (at the time a modern-day record), while McEnroe had yet to win the tennis world's most coveted title.

When these two great players entered the tennis shrine known simply as 'Centre Court' on a cool Sunday afternoon, they did so in front of an electrified stadium with hundreds of millions more watching on television. But as the match got underway it didn't appear as if it would be much of a match at all. McEnroe came out firing on all cylinders. After a mere 20 minutes of play, McEnroe had secured the first set, six games to one. McEnroe appeared to be cruising in the second set as well, holding serve with ease. Through his first nine service games McEnroe had stingily relinquished only 13 points on his serve. Yet with Borg returning serve and leading six games to five, he had a glimmer of hope. McEnroe, serving at 15-30, had let the door open a crack, and Borg, being the champion that he is, walked right through it by ripping two backhand service return winners and taking the second set 7-5. And now, as often happens in sports, the momentum had turned in an instant, and Borg capitalised by winning the third set, 6-3. At this point, Borg looked like he was going to ride the wave all the way to the title when he was serving at 5-4, 40-15, with double match point. But it was here that the inconceivable happened. Could it be that the unflappable Borg got nervous? Apparently so, as Johnny Mac fought back to break serve and even the set at five games apiece. Both players then went on to hold their serves at love.

And then it happened...the most exciting, tantalising, excruciating, nail-biting 22 minutes that tennis has ever seen. The fourth set tiebreaker started off predictably enough as the first eight points went to the server. But when Borg secured a mini break with a terrific return of serve and the players split the next two points, Borg had his third match point. As McEnroe staved it off with a stretch forehand volley winner, the crowd was in a frenzy. Little did they know that these gladiators were just getting started. On and on and on they went. With brilliant play they traded match points for set points. Finally, with Borg serving at 16-17, he could take the pressure of the moment no longer and dumped a forehand volley into the net. When all was said and done, Borg had relinquished five championship points (not to mention the two championship points he had earlier in the set) and McEnroe had finally won the tiebreaker on his seventh set point. As the crowd roared, the players tried to compose themselves on the changeover before starting the fifth and final set that would determine the champion.

At this point few people, least of all McEnroe, felt that any mere mortal could come back after losing such a heart wrenching set...not even the great Bjorn Borg. But with the heart of a lion and an iron will that legends are made of, Borg played a brilliant final set. After a hiccup that saw him lose the first two points on serve, Borg won 19 straight service points and 28 of the last 29. Yet McEnroe, who was proving to be a great champion in his own right, was matching Borg game for game, albeit with more difficulty. McEnroe came back on two occasions in the fifth set from love-40 to gallantly fight off break points. But when McEnroe was serving at 6-7, 15-40, and facing two more match points, he could play a modern-day Harry Houdini no longer. When Borg ripped one of his patented backhand passing shots past McEnroe for a clean winner and fell to his knees in triumph, it was all over. Bjorn Borg had done it again, winning his fifth straight Wimbledon.

But as the ancient Romans taught us, all fame is fleeting. Borg's glory as the monarch of the tennis world was destined to be short-lived, and McEnroe would have his revenge. A couple of months later, McEnroe defeated Borg in another classic five-setter to win his second straight US Open (see incredible moment #20). John then won his first of three Wimbledon titles by beating Borg in the 1981 Championships. And ultimately, after McEnroe was victorious once again in the 1981 US Open final, the immortal and enigmatic Bjorn Borg had apparently had enough, and retired at the age of 26.

'The Greatest Match I've Ever Seen'

Rafael Nadal v. Roger Federer

Tennis's number one most incredible moment occurred where else, but at the granddaddy of all tournaments, the Wimbledon final on 6 July 2008. Why do we love sports? What is it that truly brings us to the edge of our seats and makes us remember a fleeting moment for generations? I believe the critical factor is a great rivalry. Would Muhammad Ali be considered 'The Greatest' if it weren't for Joe Frazier? Would Evert and Navratilova be such sensational icons if they hadn't pushed each other to greater heights?

Many tennis historians have already designated Roger Federer the best to have ever played the game. Now in his early thirties, Roger has set records that may never be surpassed. But while he was building this incredible record, breezing through victory after victory, the one thing the great Federer lacked was a true rival.

Enter a Majorcan whirlwind who has the physical assets of a racehorse and the temperament of a pitbull...Rafael Nadal shocked the tennis world by winning the 2005 French Open as an 18 year old, and since then he has been a thorn in Federer's side. While Roger was dominating the rest of the tennis world, 'Rafa' was steadily building a commanding head-to-head lead over the world's Number One. But there remained one place where the Swiss Master still had his rival's number, the revered grass courts of Wimbledon, as evidenced by Federer's victories over the upstart Spaniard in the 2006 and 2007 Wimbledon Finals. Yet, coming into the 2008 Championships, many tennis pundits were predicting the unthinkable: that Federer, the five-time Wimbledon defending champion, might actually be vulnerable. By Roger's standards, he was having an off year and was in danger of giving up his number one ranking. Furthermore, Nadal was posting impressive results in the grass court warm-up tournaments, proving that he was more than a one trick, clay court pony.

As Federer and Nadal, the number one and two seeds, made their way through the tournament, the dream final was set and the sports world held its breath. As it turned out, the hype proved to be on target: The date of 6 July 2008 would be one that the 15,000 in attendance, and the millions watching around the globe, will never forget.

After a 35-minute rain delay the match got underway. It was Nadal who struck the initial blow, winning the first set in convincing fashion, 6-4. Federer seized the momentum by jumping out to a four games to one second set advantage, but incredibly, Nadal turned the tables again and won the next five games to take the set 6-4, for a commanding two-set lead.

With the infamous Wimbledon storm clouds threatening, Nadal moved in for the kill. At 3-3 in the third set Rafa held three break points when Roger served at 0-40. But Federer wasn't about to lie down, promptly reeling off five straight points to take the game. This was followed by both players holding serve...and then the rains came once more, this time resulting in an 80-minute delay.

The weather factor led to an animated exchange between the analysts. Would the interruption in play favour either player? Nadal was younger, and although Federer was considered to be in top physical shape, Nadal's physique certainly made him look physically stronger. Also, his practice sessions and workout routines were legendary for their savage ferocity.

There was also the factor of mental toughness, but this one was a draw. No one could remember even a single moment when they had witnessed, or even heard of, either of these players cracking under pressure.

The conclusion? Slight advantage to Federer. Roger was famous for never showing weakness but he had been under a lot of pressure recently, and he just might benefit from a chance to catch his breath. Also, Nadal could possibly be 'iced' by the delay. Not that he would choke, but if he had a lapse of concentration, that could conceivably allow Federer to work his way back into the match.

The speculation continued when they returned to Centre Court. Initially there were no signs that either player had gained an advantage. But shortly after play resumed the opponents found themselves in a third-set tiebreaker, and Federer seemed to come alive. With his back to the wall, Roger ramped up his aggressive game and took the breaker by a score of seven points to five.

The fourth set was more of the same: a tooth and nail struggle that once again required a deciding tiebreaker. Rafael jumped out to a five points to two advantage, but Roger continued to scrap, incredibly winning the next four points to hold set point. Now it was Rafa's turn. He staved off the set point, and then won the next as well to hold his first match point. Back and forth it went. Roger hit a service winner to pull even, but Rafa earned another match point when he held an 8-7 advantage. During match point number two, Nadal seized a short ball and attacked by ripping a forehand approach shot to Federer's weaker side, his backhand. The crowd tensed as Nadal positioned himself at net, poised for victory.

And then it happened...with the match all but over, Federer the Magician hit a jaw-dropping backhand pass down the line, then rode the momentum as well as the frenzied crowd's energy to win the next two points and the fourth set tiebreaker, ten points to eight.

Now it was the fifth and final set. Match even. Two sets apiece. Tension at fever pitch. But at two games all, cloudy darkness began to creep in and the rains came once again. It appeared that Mother Nature was gearing up to snatch away the drama, and again the speculation ensued that Federer might benefit from the reprieve. But after only 30 minutes the men were back on the court, and the battle raged on. As always, Nadal was the personification of blood and guts; sweating and grimy, a heroic, long-suffering pretender to the grass court throne. And even Federer, normally Mister Cool, looked more than a little frazzled, exhorting himself with frequent fist pumping and outbursts of 'Yes!' and 'Come on!'

As the contest continued to exact its toll, both players drew on every ounce of reserve. When the score reached seven games apiece, even the observers were exhausted, and there was no fifth-set tiebreaker! With darkness making play nearly impossible, it seemed that there would barely be time for a final two games before the match would have to be delayed. Roger struggled with his serve, saving one, two, then three break points, but the fourth proved to be fatal. The defending champion misfired on a forehand and Rafael had his crucial service break. The score was now 8-7, so after they changed sides of the court, Nadal simply needed to hold serve to preserve his first Wimbledon title...But it would not be easy. Roger maintained his extraordinary gallantry, holding off a third match point...

And then it happened...again... 'The King is dead, long live the King!' The embattled Federer hit one last forehand into the net as Rafael Nadal fell to the ground in triumph. When all was said and done the match was the longest in Wimbledon finals history, lasting four hours and 48 minutes and ending at 9.15 pm. Furthermore, the loss ended Federer's grass-court winning streak at 65 straight, and the victory made Nadal the first man to win the French Open and Wimbledon back-to-back since the great Bjorn Borg pulled it off in 1980. After the match Rafael, in his charming, Spanish-accented English, told BBC Sport, 'It's impossible to explain what I felt in that moment but I'm very, very happy. It is a dream to play on this court, my favourite tournament, but to win I never imagined.' And for his part, announcer John McEnroe, who played in what was previously deemed to be the tennis match for the ages (see incredible moment #2), concluded with a short but profound summation:

'This was the greatest match I've ever seen.'

Bonus Stories

Since the original printing of *101 Incredible Moments In Tennis* in 2010, our beautiful sport has continued to amaze. It seems with each passing year, the tennis world has been producing monumental moments at an astonishing pace. As a result, there were literally nearly a dozen moments that were worthy of consideration in a book delineating incredible tennis moments. Yet, after careful consideration, I have decided to include only the following three matches, each of which, in my humble opinion, are worthy of consideration as a top moment in the history of tennis. I hope you, the tennis enthusiast, enjoy reading these bonus stories as much as I cherished writing them.

Seventy-Seven Years

Andy Murray v. Novak Djokovic

Tennis's first incredible 'bonus' moment occurred at the 2013 Wimbledon final. Everyone loves a hometown hero. Whatever the venue, it's thrilling to see one of your own do great things on an international stage, and our exciting sport of tennis is no exception. Whether it's the Australian Open, French Open, U.S. Open, or in this case Wimbledon, the host country will always yearn for a compatriot to hold its nation's crown jewel.

So it was no surprise that, during the 2013 Wimbledon Championships, the British fans were hoping for one of their own to take home the title. And who could blame them? A British man had not hoisted the Wimbledon trophy since Fred Perry did so in 1936, seventy-seven years earlier. No doubt many a British fan would have gladly made a contract with the devil to insure the rightful return of this coveted prize to a native son.

During those seventy-seven years without a British winner, there had been several near misses between long stretches of utter futility. Only two years after Perry's triumph, Bunny Austin was the tournament's runner-up. In 1961, Mike Sangster was a semi-finalist but could advance no further. In 1963, Bobby Wilson was a quarter-finalist. The big serving lefty, Roger Taylor, was knocking on the door when he reached the semi-finals in 1967, 1970, and 1973, but each of these ended in heartbreaking losses. The Brits were so desperate that they gladly accepted the Canadian transport turned UK citizen, Greg Rusedski, but the man with the perfect serve for grass only made the quarters on one occasion. And of course who could forget Tim Henman. Tim reached four semi-finals but could never get over the hump to have a chance at the crown.

And then there was Andy Murray. The Scot was clearly Britain's best player since Perry, and after losing in the finals to the great Roger Federer in four hard fought sets during the 2012 championships, the tennis world knew that he would be back, especially after his tearful "I'm getting closer" lament in the post match interview.

Entering the 2013 fortnight, 'Murray Mania' was palpable. And when Rafael Nadal lost in the first round, and defending champion, Roger Federer, lost in the second, the draw had opened up. Although Andy seemed to be in good form through the early rounds, the mounting pressure for him to bring home the title was overwhelming. Could this be Andy's (and the United Kingdom's) best chance for victory for the conceivable future? With Murray cruising into the quarter-finals all was going according to form. But when he met up with Spain's Fernando Verdasco he was soon in a pressure cooker, down two sets, 6-4 and 6-3. Suddenly it was do or die, and Andy Murray was not about to die. To the delight of the British faithful, he roared back to take the final three sets, 6-1, 6-4, 7-5. And after taking out Poland's Jerzy Janowicz in four sets in the semis, Andy was once again on immortality's doorstep. But the last hurdle was by far the biggest: past Wimbledon champion Novak Djokovic.

On the final Sunday, the two superstars walked into Centre Court's sweltering heat to play for the title. Physical conditioning and mental fortitude would be major factors. And with "The Joker's" history of six grand slam wins, the advantage appeared to be his. But as the match proceeded, it was Djokovic who seemed to be melting under the pressure. Andy took the first set six games to four, but the unflappable Novak roared back to take a commanding four games to one lead in the second. Yet Andy would not be deterred. He turned the tables to take the set, seven games to five, and now had a commanding two sets to love advantage. In what seemed like déjà vu, Djokovic sprinted ahead in the third set as well, this time by four games to two. But once again, Murray showed his steel. He broke serve, held, and broke again to go up five games to four.

Now both Andy and his frenzied fans were hoping for an easy game, and the first three points went as planned. With Murray up 40-love and the stadium noise at a deafening pitch, it was all but over. But no one seemed to tell the Serb, who won not one, not two, not three, but *four* straight points.

Suddenly a nightmare scenario dawned. Just a few moments after being a point away from the title, Murray was actually *down* a break point! If he lost this game it would be a crushing blow. His spirit would surely be broken, and Djokovic might well run off the last three sets.

The Great British Hope looked as if he might pass out on the court. But he somehow managed to fight off the break point, only to face another, and then a third! Ten excruciating minutes passed from the time he had a 40-love lead. Finally there came a brilliant defensive point, giving Murray a fourth match point to become Wimbledon champion.

And then it happened...Djokovic netted a backhand, the crowd roared, and Murray raised his arms in triumph. The seventy-seven-year wait was finally over. Andy Murray was the champion of Wimbledon, and all of Great Britain celebrated into the night and beyond. Well done, Andy. Well done.

Warriors

Novak Djokovic v. Rafael Nadal

Tennis's second incredible 'bonus' moment occurred in the Australian Open final in 2012. In my opinion, tennis is one of the most difficult sports to play at the highest level, and I'm not referring to the demanding athleticism, the physical conditioning, or the lightning reflexes that are required to endure hours of intense competition, often under blazing heat. My rationale is that tennis demands a level of mental strength unlike any other sport. Once a player steps onto the court, he or she is all alone. No coach, no moral support, no teammates to share not only the disappointment of defeat, but worse, the responsibility for it. The emotional burden can be crushing, so much so that only a select group can handle it on a given day, and even fewer can do so with consistency.

It is generally accepted that the world's top one hundred players are pretty much evenly matched in terms of basic talent and stroke production. For that matter, even at the level of a division one college match, the level of play can be mind boggling. So how is it that year after year, a small handful of contenders are a virtual lock to make it to the quarters and semis of every big tournament?

The answer? Those elite few have a different mindset. They know they can win. They *plan* to win. They *expect* to win.

You know the names: Coming into the 2012 Australian Open, the big three, Roger Federer, Rafael Nadal, and the world's number one at that time, Novak Djokovic had been dominating the game, with Scotland's Andy Murray knocking on the door. So it was not a surprise when these four warriors found themselves battling it out in the semi-finals of the year's first grand slam.

In the semis, Nadal defeated Federer in four hard fought sets. But it was nothing compared to Djokovic's effort, who needed five grueling sets to dismiss Murray in a match that lasted four hours and fifty minutes. With that kind of exhausting effort, the smart money assumed that Novak wouldn't last if the match went past three sets.

As the final began, things went from bad to worse for the already weary Djokovic when Nadal took the first set seven games to five. Although Novak had defeated Nadal in the two previous grand slam finals, it was common knowledge that the Spaniard was a great front-runner, and when Rafa took the first set in a grand slam match, he was nearly unstoppable. In fact, Nadal's record was 133-1 when winning the first set in the four majors. But Djokovic had the mental strength to dismiss the stats, fighting back to take the next two sets 6-4, and 6-2. However, even though he was now down two sets to one, Nadal knew that if he could somehow manage to win the fourth set, the pendulum would swing back in his favor. As it turned out, the fourth set went to a tiebreaker and Djokovic grabbed a commanding 5-2 lead. The finish line was in sight, but now it was time for Rafael to show his steel, and in a stunning display, he reeled off five straight points to take the fourth set.

Now it was a one set contest for the championship. As the match went deep into the night, the riveted crowd watched as Nadal made the first move, breaking in game six to gain a four games to two advantage. But with a thirty-fifteen lead on his own serve in the following game, Rafa missed an easy backhand and Djokovic seized the opportunity to break serve, then held his own serve to tie things up at four games all. After both men held serve for five all, Novak struck again to break in the eleventh game. Nadal would illustrate his tenacity when he fought to earn a break point of his own, but the cool Serb held on and came back to reach championship point.

And then it happened... With a big serve up the middle, Djokovic put away Nadal's return and it was over. The two warriors had played the longest match in the history of the Australian Open, and the longest grand slam final in the history of the open era. The official time: Five hours and fifty-three minutes!

After the match, Rafa called the contest the toughest loss of his career, but the best match he had ever played. For his part, Novak said it was the finest win of his career. And in case these sentiments weren't convincing enough, former tennis legends Bjorn Borg, Mats Wilander, Pete Sampras, Andre Agassi, and Goran Ivanisevic all stated that it was the best match they ever saw. That about sums it up.

Rest In Peace, Mr. Van Alen

John Isner v. Nicolas Mahut

Tennis's third incredible 'bonus' moment occurred at the 2010 Wimbledon Championships. In 1965, James Van Alen invented the tennis tiebreaker in an effort to control the length of matches. Prior to the tiebreak, all sets had to be won by a margin of two games. And after a monumental five hour and twelve minute Wimbledon struggle between Pancho Gonzalez and Charlie Pasarell, resulting in a 22-24, 1-6, 16-14, 6-3, 11-9 victory for the 41-year-old Gonzalez (see incredible moment #55), the British tennis authorities began to give Van Alen's tiebreak some serious consideration. Eventually, in 1979, the big 'W' changed it rules so that the tiebreak would take effect, except in the final set, where the players still had to win by the traditional two game margin.

Forty-five years after Van Alen's brainstorm, Nicolas Mahut was vying for a place in the main draw at the Championships. The Frenchman would have to fight his way through the qualifying tournament if he hoped to earn his ticket to the main event. Nicolas started off well by defeating Frank Danevic 6-3, 6-0. But if he thought he was going to cakewalk his way through the qualifiers he was in for a dose of reality. In the very next round he found himself in an epic struggle with Alex Bogdanovic, barely managing to survive with a cliffhanger 3-6, 6-3, 24-22 victory. And it wasn't going to get easier. Needing to win one more match to earn his way into the main draw, this time a five setter, Mahut lost the first two sets to Stefan Koubek 6-7(8), 3-6 before rallying back to win the last three by the scores of 6-3, 6-4, 6-4.

At last he had earned an appearance in at the big dance of Wimbledon, where he drew the American John Isner in the first round on court eighteen. While he was undoubtedly thrilled to get through qualifying, Mahut was still hoping to make some noise in the main draw.

The Isner-Mahut match started on the fortnight's second day. Although there was a late start, darkness doesn't fully envelop the Wimbledon grounds until slightly after 9:00 pm local time, so it was likely that the contest would finish up by day's end. But so much for probabilities. After the American won the first set 6-4, the Frenchman took the second and third sets, 6-3 and 7-6, respectively. Then, when Isner evened the match by winning the fourth set in a tiebreak of his own, the match was suspended due to darkness.

When the combatants came out the next day to finish the match, they both assumed it would be one quick set until the outcome was finalized. But this one didn't go according to the script. Both men were holding serve with ease, and with no tiebreak in the final set at Wimbledon, they would go on...and on...and on! 6 all, 8 all, 10 all; 20, 30, 40! Finally, at 59-59, the match was suspended for a second time.

When they came out on June 24th for their unfathomable third day of battle, they had already played the longest match in the history of the game!

And then it happened...finally, mercifully, after 65 minutes of play on that historic third day, Isner broke Mahut with a backhand pass down the line, securing the victory by a score of 70 games to 68!

After all was said and done, the longest match of all time took an eye-popping eleven hours and five minutes! The fifth set alone, at eight hours and eleven minutes, was longer than any other entire match ever played! The fifth set took 138 games, and the entire match took 183 games... obviously both records. Isner recorded the most aces ever in one match at 113. And Mahut's total ace count was 103 (the second most of all time). Ironically, it would be Mahut who, despite losing, ended up with the most points won in a match at 502.

The length of this one remarkable match was longer than the entire amount of time it took Serena Williams to win all seven of her matches in the previous year's tournament on her way to the title. And in case you were wondering, the exhausted Isner lost his very next round to the unheralded Thiemo de Bakker 0-6, 3-6, 2-6 in just seventy-four minutes, which was the shortest match to that point of the 2010 Championships. And because the tennis gods apparently have a sense of humor, in the very next year, at the 2011 Wimbledon tournament, Isner and Mahut drew each other again in - you guessed it - the very first round. But this time Isner won in straight sets, 7-6, 6-2, 7-6 in a mere two hours three minutes.

One can only imagine that Jimmy Van Alen, who passed on 3 July 1991, was turning over in his grave during that interminable final set. But I say, 'Not to worry, Mr. Van Alen. The lack of a fifth set tiebreaker at Wimbledon has led, at least in this case, to a match for the ages.'

About the Author

Joshua Shifrin

Joshua Shifrin has been teaching tennis on a full- or part-time basis for nearly 25 years. Dr. Shifrin has been a high school tennis coach and the co-number one player for his state championship high school tennis team as well as the number one singles and doubles player for Clark University in Massachusetts. Dr. Shifrin lives with his wife and sons in New Jersey. Dr. Shifrin is a licensed psychologist and continues to enjoy playing, watching and writing about tennis at every opportunity.

Printed in Great Britain
by Amazon